THE COMPLETE
Pebble Mosaic
HANDBOOK

THE COMPLETE
Pebble Mosaic
HANDBOOK

REVISED AND EXPANDED

Maggy Howarth

FIREFLY BOOKS

Author's note on measurements
I always use metric measurements (given in brackets in the text). In my opinion, they
are the most precise choice. The Imperial equivalents given are as near as possible
and should be followed until you have some experience. Then you may find it easier
to round up or down to simpler fractions, according to the kind of work you are doing
and the size of pebbles you are using.

A Firefly Book

Published by Firefly Books Ltd. 2009

First Printing

Publisher Cataloging-in-Publication Data (U.S.)

Howarth, Maggy.
    The complete pebble mosaic handbook / Maggy Howarth.
Originally published, 2003.
[256] p. : col. photos. ; cm.
Includes bibliographical references and index.
Summary: An illustrated guide for creating basic to advanced pebble mosaic projects. Includes
tips on design, how to find or buy the best pebbles and examples of work from pebble mosaic
artists around the world.
ISBN-13: 978-1-55407-418-1 (pbk.)
ISBN-10: 1-55407-418-5 (pbk.)
1. Pebble mosaics. 2. Pavements, Mosaic. 3. Mosaic floors.   I. Title.
738.52 dc22   NA3810.H69 2008

Library and Archives Canada Cataloguing in Publication

Howarth, Maggy
    The complete pebble mosaic handbook / Maggy Howarth. -- 2nd ed.

Includes bibliographical references and index.
ISBN-13: 978-1-55407-418-1
ISBN-10: 1-55407-418-5

        1. Pebble mosaics--Technique. 2. Mosaics--Technique. I. Title.

TT910.H69 2008   738.5   C2008-900757-3

Published in the United States by
Firefly Books (U.S.) Inc.
P.O.Box 1338, Ellicott Station
Buffalo, New York 14205

Published in Canada by
Firefly Books Ltd.
66 Leek Crescent
Richmond Hill, Ontario L4B 1H1

Design by Shelley Watson/Sublime Design
Printed in China through Colorcraft Ltd., Hong Kong

CONTENTS

FOREWORD

This new edition brings a fresh look at some aspects of the art of pebble mosaics: new artists, new developments and new materials. In the last four years I have acquired a role as information gatherer, archivist and facilitator, putting artists, craftsmen and technicians in contact with each other across the world — in addition to responding to pleas for advice. So, there's plenty of news! It's a pleasure to show you some recent pebble mosaics that have been made all over the world, by both professional artists and enthusiastic amateurs.

Catching the pebble "bug" can be life-changing: conscious of our mortality we grasp at the idea of permanence. There is a spiritual satisfaction to be gained from the careful placing of natural stones in rhythmic patterns and bonding them together like fossils in a lava flow. There is a basic appeal in the pebble as a found object, formed by the great forces of nature, recalling memories of happy childhood days spent on sunny beaches. We are naturally drawn to the smoothness of rounded stone; it's a small and perfect emblem of the earth we walk on. When we pick up a pebble and marvel at its beauty, we are holding a chunk of our planet; and when we pick up handfuls, and arrange them together in patterns, we are reflecting the universe. Children love to do it; so do adults, if they give themselves the time to play. Some take it one step further, to make their collection of stones into something more permanent: designing, making and then leaving for posterity a pebble mosaic.

However, even for the long-lived mosaic, times are changing. Today, imported pebbles from the Far East have become widely available and have altered the appearance and color of pebblework and, to some extent, our attitude. I regret the loss of those long days on the beach or the riverbank, searching for pristine and perfect material. Collecting our own pebbles brings a local distinctiveness to the craft, impossible to reproduce with foreign imports. But we have to use what we can get and, at least for the moment, the imports seem to be endless, whereas our own supplies are increasingly protected or unavailable.

There have been other changes too. Commercial products such as "pebble tiles" have become widely available. They are cheap and cheerful and presented as a fashionable design solution, less permanent by nature, but more easily and cheaply achieved than the hand-made original genre. While we must recognize the trend, and to some extent adjust to the influence of fashion, I hope that the reader will once more indulge me as I bang the drum for the *best* and *only the best* in pebble mosaic. No half-measures.

Design is everything! At the end of the day it is the designs with real artistic merit which will be valued and preserved. And good design for pebble mosaic means precise drawing, making use of the special shapes and properties of natural pebbles, and giving due consideration to the context in which the mosaic is to be placed. Within these guidelines, the solutions are endless. I never cease to be amazed at the variety of effects produced with the same materials by different artists and craftsmen.

Bear in mind that it is never too late to change the design while it is still on paper. The process of making a mosaic is so laborious and time-consuming that it pays to be absolutely sure that the design is the best that you can do.

Make it last! I must enter a plea for permanence. It takes an effort of will and great patience to maintain the highest standards of durability in materials and construction; but a mosaic of real beauty which will also last for hundreds of years is our ultimate aim.

So, what you will see in this book is the best of pebble mosaic. The examples have been chosen on the basis that they are either original or inventive, or otherwise interesting for some aspect of their material construction. What we all know as "worthy projects" have not been included. Also, "complete" editions are never truly complete, and I hope to continue to gather information and bring it into the public domain in the future.

My courses and workshops in the art of pebble mosaic are documented here. I know that people love to have personal one-on-one teaching, and the experience has also been rewarding for me. But it is my hope that the newly inspired will be brave enough to learn from the step-by-step sequences in this book without recourse to expensive workshop tuition. Many have done so from my previous books.

All newcomers to the art are welcome to make use of designs in Section 3 as a starting-point for their work; although (please!) not for profit. Having gained experience and confidence, when you go on to make your own designs, do let me see your creations. I am always interested and forever thankful.

Maggy Howarth

Thanks

A huge thank you to **Boris Howarth**, who has patiently edited and improved the text of this book, and been my enthusiastic companion and cameraman on our many journeys in search of pebble mosaics.

To **Mark Currie**, my long-time assistant, whose loyalty and meticulous craftsmanship have been crucial to  developing the craft of pebble mosaics at Cobblestone Designs workshop.

To the artists and craftsmen in this book, who have been so generous in sharing information about their processes and materials. I am sure that the free exchange of ideas between craftsmen can only be to everyone's benefit and help to nurture the network of enthusiasts for pebble mosaic.

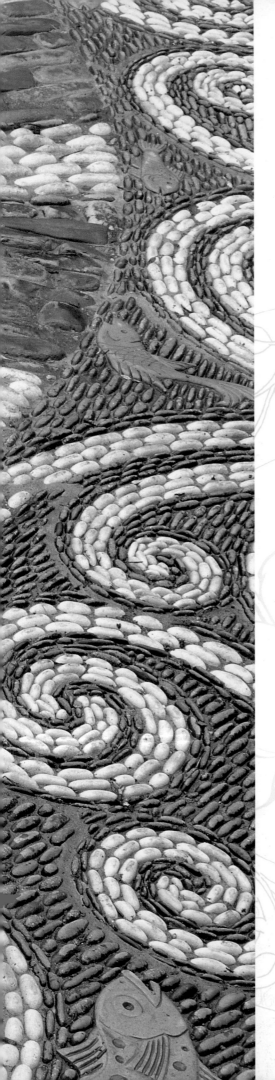

Section **1**

Core
Techniques

1 THE BASIC PRINCIPLES

First things first: let's take a look at the basic principles of good practice that will turn an assemblage of pebbles into a hard surface that is durable and permanent. A thorough understanding of these principles—in terms of technique, materials and design—is necessary before setting out to make a pebble mosaic.

TECHNIQUE

In *The Art of Pebble Mosaics* four rules underlying the construction of pebble mosaics are described. They are repeated here because they are so important. Sticking to these principles of physical construction is the only way to ensure the strength of the mosaic. Cement may lend added security, but it cannot replace correct technique.

A pebble mosaic in cross-section showing the four basic rules underlying the construction of pebble mosaics: a solid base, side restraints, pebbles set vertically and pebbles tightly packed.

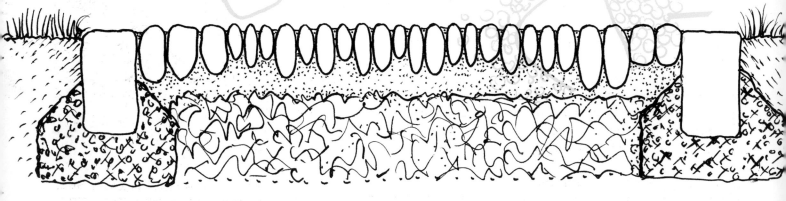

The base
A mosaic needs a foundation just the same as a house. It must be absolutely solid. It can be a concrete foundation, or compact aggregate consolidated with a vibrating roller; and its thickness must be sufficient for the weight that the mosaic must withstand.

Side restraint
Pebbles will break away from the edges of the mosaic unless adequate side restraint is provided. A curb or wall may already exist but, if not, a good border should be formed with stone or brick, bedded on mortar.

Pebbles set vertically
Like the teeth in your jaw, pebbles should always be placed vertically—*never* flat.

Tight packing
Use pebbles shaped like flat disks, cylinders or blocks so that they can be packed *tightly together:* locked one against the other so that they cannot be dislodged.

MATERIALS

Hardness
Use pebbles that are so hard they cannot be crushed or shattered, cracked or chipped. If in doubt, test them with a hammer. Most fine-grained pebbles found on beaches are usable as the continuous pounding of the waves reduces softer stones to sand, leaving only the hardest. Commonly these will be granites, slate, hard limestones, fine-grained sandstones, quartz and flint.

There are several types, however, which ought to be rejected. Coarse, grainy sandstones don't wear well, and their surfaces encourage green algae. Stones with holes and cracks will be weak and unsightly. Beware also broken bricks that masquerade as attractive warm red pebbles. They might look pretty, but they shouldn't be used as they break up in frost.

Collecting your own pebbles
Finding a good source of pebbles is half the battle. Beaches, rivers and quarries are the main hunting grounds, but there are legal restrictions, which will vary

⬆ *Before collecting your own pebbles, check that there are no legal restrictions on access and removal of stones.*

*Good and bad stones for pebble mosaic
Good stones: (top row, from left) white quartz, yellow quartz, hard black dolerite, fine-grained hard sandstone, white limestone; (second row) four colors of granite, flint.*

Bad stones: (third row, from left) soft grainy sandstone, a group of cracked stones, tumbled white marble (too porous); (bottom row, from left) worn glass fragment (soft and splintery), a "pebble" that is actually a worn piece of porous soft brick, some very veiny quartz that shatters easily, and a group of Indonesian stones, which are all porous and susceptible to frost damage.

from country to country. All foreshores belong to somebody: a landowner, an organization or even the state. To stay within the law, this owner must be identified and permission sought for both access and the removal of stone. It would be unusual for anyone to object to an amateur mosaicist collecting a small quantity by hand. In fact, large shingly beaches are sometimes considered a nuisance, their pebbles shifted by rogue tides and spilt dangerously across walkways. So it's always worth asking. Ecologically and environmentally sensitive sites must be avoided, for obvious reasons.

Permission must also be obtained for river banks. They too can be a good source of material, especially where the river flows through a glacial deposit. Such deposits are sometimes excavated by quarries. Ask nicely, and they may allow you to select from their stockpiles and buy the results.

It may be that access is denied to some beaches and in this case, buying may be the only option.

Different shapes of pebble

It's useful to classify the pebbles you collect into different shape types: longs, cylinders, flat-tops and specials.

Longs or *skimmers* are thin flying-saucer shapes; wonderfully expressive. They will give flowing lines and many patterns.

Cylinders are rounded and long shapes, which will make an allover texture. They are useful in creating different patterns and can also suggest scaly forms.

Flat-tops are like a head with a flat crown, but often angular; these make a different texture. They can be of a larger size than you might normally use, creating intriguing contrasts with the smaller pebbles.

Specials are odd stones that you can't help picking up. Banded stones that have a ring of a different color in

A selection of pebbles for mosaic

Longs or Skimmers:
1 Maroon hard sandstones from India; 2 hard gray river sandstones; 3 red granite; 4, 5, 6, 7 unpolished Chinese blacks, plum reds, whites and yellows.

Flat-tops:
8 Big stones for effect; 9 hard river sandstone; 10 red granite; 11 mixed glacial material.

Cylinders:
12 Black basalt; 13 white limestone; 14 pink granite.

Strips and Chunks:
15 Irregular slivers of riven slate; 16 angular quarried limestone chunks; 17 various sections of curved and flat stoneware tile and pipe; 18 brown flints of all shapes.

Colors, Specials and Exotics:
Special shapes and "finds" such as the 19 worn stoneware bottle-rim; 20 yellow and red "jasper" or cherts; 21 some attractive rare green and jewel-like stones; 22 white, yellow and veined quartz; 23 a collection of "eyes" encircled by shards of black porcelain and 24 white ceramic "pins;" 25 glass nuggets and 26 marbles; 27 ceramic grinding material or alumina; 28 green quartz gravel; 29 yellow pea gravel.

Exotic stones sourced as rough rocks and then tumbled:
30 Green amazonite; 31 blue dumortierite; 32 mauve amethyst; 33 dark blue sodalite; and 34 spotted leopard rhyolite.

The groups are separated by cut slate strips and riven slate of various colors.

The shapes of pebbles and the textures they will make

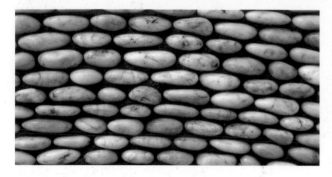

Flat pebbles — "Longs" or "Skimmers" These are the most expressive pebbles. They give flow and direction to a design. To create a basic weave with longs, off-set the pebbles in rows, as in brickwork, and keep the width of each line constant: making "fat" rows and "thin" rows. Many patterns are possible, such as the sun border (above right). A good effect is made by gradually reducing the width of the pebbles in the rows to make diminishing or radiating lines (far right). In practice, you need to add in a line occasionally. In this case, strips of slate make crisp lines. A herringbone pattern (right) makes an expressive frond.

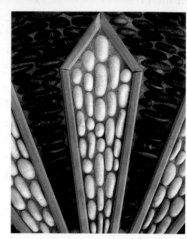

Cylinders or "Rounds" These make an attractive all-over texture. A range of sizes is needed in order to fit them together without gaps. Pick the size to fit the space. When graded for size, cylinders make attractive patterns (see above right).

Quarry stone Crushed rock from quarries is angular and has to be selected for suitable shapes. It can be a useful "filler."

Flat-tops Some stones naturally form block-shaped pebbles which can be selected for their long tooth-like shape and flat top. They make a pleasant random texture that contrasts well with the longs. Flat-tops are good for scaly effects or, as above, a flower.

Gravel "Pea" gravel is rounded like miniature pebbles and can be used like exposed aggregate in mosaic, or pressed into wet mortar as a contrasting texture.

their center are worth collecting to use as eyes. Similarly, bright-colored stones, though hard to find in quantity, will come in handy for jewel-like details against a background of plainer stone.

Buying pebbles

At the time of writing, imported stones are becoming increasingly available. They can be ordered from around the world and shipped direct. However, their quality often leaves a lot to be desired, the selection is rarely good enough and the percentage of the pebbles that are the right shape for pebble mosaic can be low.

All these points will need to be checked. However, I expect that bringing pebbles from other countries will increase in the future, and that we will learn with practice what are the best materials and how to use them.

⬆ *Waterworn sandstones from the river are being sorted for the Wray mosaic. It saves time to have well-sorted materials already on hand when you come to placing the stones. At the same time, cracked, soft and stained stones can be picked out and discarded.*

Other kinds of stone material

Various commercial gravels are readily obtainable from building supply stores. The best type for associating with pebbles is pea gravel, a natural waterworn material. It is especially useful for work with children, who love to use these miniature pebbles to fill in the gaps between the larger ones.

Crushed quarry stone can be another useful material, if the shapes are carefully selected. Their angular surfaces can be fitted together, and will contrast well with waterworn pebbles. It is a technique much used in China to very good effect.

Sawn stone for cutting and carving can often be bought cheaply as offcuts from quarries that produce stone in blocks. Suitable pieces must be selected by hand, and will probably be charged by weight. Stonemasons' yards are another source for small pieces of stone.

Non-stone materials

Some man-made materials associate well with natural pebbles. Ceramic shards and tiles are useful, but must be fired to stoneware temperature or they will crack in frost. Glass should be used with care, as it is often quite soft and can splinter easily. Glass "nuggets" and marbles are satisfactory in protected situations with light foot traffic. Colored glass "smalti," a vitreous mosaic material, is attractive but soft, and should be used sparingly.

Different countries and different localities will all yield special individual products that may be of use, but they must be both hard and nonporous. Use all of these man-made materials with caution: too many artificial colors and unnatural textures can result in some very garish effects.

DESIGNING PEBBLE MOSAICS

Remember that, given the choice, most of us prefer our everyday walking to take place on a smooth surface, so that we don't always have to look where we're going. A pebble pavement should be reserved for places where something special is called for; where care and skill in design and making will reflect the importance of the particular location. It should be a focal point, but always placed where pedestrians can choose to walk around it.

A pebble mosaic is always affected by its surroundings, associating well with natural stone paving slabs and bricks, but visually uncomfortable in association with concrete and asphalt because their lack of natural divisions presents too great a contrast in texture. Equally difficult surrounds are gravel and grass, which will tend to invade from the edges; and the proximity of trees will present problems of dampness and leaf-fall. Ideal locations are open spaces where wind, sun and rain act as natural cleaning and drying agents.

Designing should never be done in isolation. The context is everything. Become familiar with the space, its colors and textures and materials; and take time to learn the resonances it holds for other people. All this will give you a context in which to dream and come up with the kernel of an idea. Then you'll need to ask some more precise questions.

So simple and right. A plain limestone path in Shizilin Garden, Suzhou, made with care and tailored between the precious characterful rocks which Chinese garden-makers love so much. With the graceful bamboos, a complete landscape picture is created.

Size
Deciding the size of a motif or pattern needs care. It's difficult to get a clear impression of some motifs unless they are big enough. You can manage to make a daisy look like a daisy with just a few long pebbles for petals and a round one at the center. But try a bird, and you need much more information for it to be at all recognizable. Even a small bird like a robin will be most effective if you actually make it the size of a chicken.

The drawing
Making a drawing before you start is invaluable. It's not a good idea to improvise at this stage; save that for the pebble details.

If you draw your design to the actual size that the mosaic is going to be, you'll be able to test whether the pebbles you intend to use will fit the design.

It's a common mistake to try to make a design which is too small for the size of pebbles to hand. Consequently, you end up searching for smaller and smaller pebbles to realize the idea, to the point where it gets impractical and frustrating.

If your design is larger than the largest paper that you have, you will need to make a scale drawing: a 1:10 ratio is the easiest. At this scale you can sketch actual pebbles on your drawing, and you will be able to tell whether the motif or pattern is the right size.

Drafting up to size
From the 1:10 scale original, draw a grid of 1 in (2.5 cm) squares onto the design. On another piece of paper, as large as the finished mosaic, draw a grid of 10 in (25 cm) squares for every 1 in (2.5 cm) of the original. Then systematically copy the lines of the original to each large square.

Materials
The pebbles that are available will greatly influence your choice of design. Their precise quality will suggest certain themes. Very marbly quartz, large and lumpy, is my favorite for fish scales. Spotty granites are wonderfully suggestive for a bird's plumage. Hard-to-find green stones are effective for the patterning of a frog or snake.

Practicalities will often dictate a choice: whether it is possible to obtain *enough* stones of a certain type to be able to carry out the idea you have in mind.

Viewpoint
How much of the mosaic can you see? This depends on where the viewer is standing: at ground level, on a balcony or on a tower. A large mosaic design can only be seen as a whole from a high viewpoint. On the ground, you can only take in a radius of around 7 ft (2 m). Try it! The rest is out of focus at the edge of your vision, so the only way to view each part is by walking over it. Designs for large mosaics must therefore be considered from both the overall viewpoint and the smaller focus points within it.

If a mosaic will be seen from a variety of viewpoints, it should not be designed with a definite top or bottom. Motifs which twist and turn, with a variety of interest from all directions, are to be aimed for.

The right thing for the place
Color is so important! In a stone-built environment choose pebbles that tone with the color of the predominant stone: warm tones for sandstone, gray and white for limestone. Try to get the mosaic looking as if it always belonged there. Touches of "foreign" material for contrast and highlights are OK, but the general effect should be one of a more detailed and refined texture than that of the environment. The general rule is to try to use local material for most of the mosaic.

I have often had to make a mosaic for a busy shopping center with flashy storefronts, bright paint colors and lighting, in an environment of plastic, metal, glass, brick … you name it!

There's no point in being too subtle here: go for maximum contrast, bright-colored stones and interesting materials. And make it strong: there's bound to be a lot of heavy use, vehicles and pollutants.

◆ Texture *There's a strong contrast of color here: bright white and black. There's also a strong contrast of texture: large irregular whites against flowing lines of black longs. Incidentally, this is a great way of using quartz, which is such a hard material that it never wears into even-sized shapes. Spacing out the larger stones and packing the smaller ones around as evenly as possible has exploited this characteristic and made it into a pattern.* DETAIL FROM THE MOSAIC AT BURTON AGNES HALL, YORKSHIRE, U.K., BY NATURESCAPE.

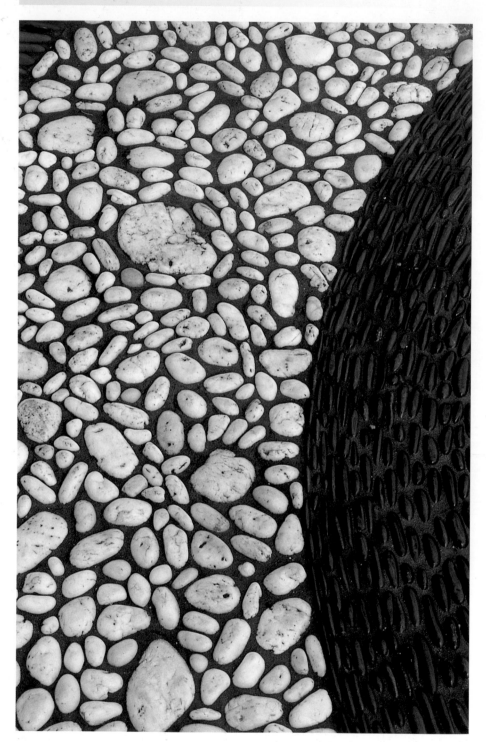

◆ Contrast *To make this little wren, the tiniest of specially selected, thin creamy flints were chosen, mingled with a few thin reds and browns with slivers of black slate to denote the feathers. The grayish white background is not very different in tone from the wren's breast, but the contrast in size of pebbles and the all-over rounded pattern make the little bird clear.* MADE BY MARK CURRIE TO A DESIGN BY MAGGY HOWARTH.

◆ Contrasting sizes *Brilliant use of large scalelike stones; gaps are filled with small material.* DETAIL FROM THE SNAKE MOSAIC BY FABRIZIO CHIOSTRINI.

⬆ *Making a 3-D effect* The pebbles are thinner at the edges of the form, gradually increasing in thickness towards the center where really large, increasingly fat stones are used. It's a subtle effect, but when it's combined with shading of the stone color, it gives a "rounded" quality to the subject.
"BULL" MADE BY JANETTE IRELAND TO DESIGN BY MAGGY HOWARTH.

⬇ *Radiating lines* In this example the rows in the foreground are tapered to a central point: a simple device, but one that always looks effective on the ground. Of course, you have to work it all out beforehand, get the pebbles well sorted and stick to the plan. Offsetting the pebbles in the rows is essential good practice.

⬇ *Shading* A nice 3-D effect can be achieved if stones are graded through several tones. In this shell design there are six tones: white, white-gray, light gray-green, green, dark green, black. You have to select stones carefully for each category (best done when they're wet) and then take care to keep each tone separate while you are working. The shading here was complicated by the curving pebble rows which were intended to emphasize the shape of the scallops. The gray tones make a nice contrast to the brilliant jewel colors of quartz and jasper, especially under water.

⬆ *Color grading* The design is simple but the color effect is lovely. There are lines of red granite, brown flints, buff granites, strong yellow, pale yellow and bright white quartzes. The sun design contrasts with the black background. Many other combinations could be used according to what's available. Even a rainbow can be achieved using exotic tumbled stones for the blues and greens.

◀ *Natural tones* Really subtle colors are natural to pebbles, although they're not always available in the right sizes and sufficient quantity to do what you want. But even small collections of very particular tones come in handy for special tasks: like trying to suggest the colors and feather textures of the eagle. Brownish black, plum colors, cream and buff flints were all used, along with more-easily available black, white and brown flints. Lots of fun!

Cut stone and slate strips

Sometimes you just can't do it with pebbles. Hard-edged lines, whether straight or curved, are nearly impossible to make with such smoothly rounded material. In situations where this effect is needed, flat slabs of stone can be cut into straight narrow strips like rulers. If the line has to be curved, then the strip can be broken every so often to make an arc. Slate is a good material for this because it has a cleaving layered structure, and the strips can be cracked against its grain and reassembled to make a continuous curve. Much practice is needed! Cut the strips about 1¹/₄ in (3 cm) wide from not too thick slabs (about ¹/₂ in or 1.2 cm is right).

You may be lucky and find a source of strips like this at a stone yard that processes roofing slate; otherwise the best way to cut these strips is with a small masonry saw, which can be rented. The "grain" of the slate lies horizontal to the slab. Crack each strip methodically at ¹/₂–2 in (1.2–5 cm) intervals (depending on the steepness of the curve you want to make). In our workshop we have a nifty device which does the job beautifully. It's an old fly-press that has been adapted to hold a cold chisel and bring it down with a two-ton point pressure. When we first started doing this, all we had was a convenient hole in the floor and handheld tools. The quality of the slate is what is most important: it should be even-textured, and without any quartz impurities.

↻ *Cut stone and slate strips* The lines of the waves have been made from strips of slate, cracked against the grain and "bent" to form curves. Tapering the strips has added to the effect. The lightning in the picture is cut from French limestone, which is difficult to work with because of its brittle structure, but is otherwise a good, hard, bright white stone. "Wind and Weather" mosaic at Gresgarth Hall.

⬆ *Even a tiny fish makes an interesting detail. The shape was cut out in slate using the masonry saw, and all the detail was worked with a 4 in (10 cm) angle grinder with various diamond disks. The usual rules apply to the selection of stone for carving: it should be hard and nonporous so that staining and weathering are kept to a minimum.*

Carving bas-relief details

A carved detail, such as a sharp beak for a bird or horn for a sheep, can add a lot of interest to the mosaic. Sometimes the size of a leaf or a claw is just too small for it to be satisfactorily made from pebbles. Cutting and carving a section of stone and working it into the main body of pebblework can be a good solution.

The required shape is first traced onto the stone. The stone should be at least 1¼ in (3 cm) thick. Cutting out the shape is most easily achieved with a masonry saw with a diamond blade, but can also be done with an angle grinder. We use the smallest standard 4 in (10 cm) angle grinder with a selection of diamond disks for cutting, grinding and smoothing. A lot of effects can be created using this tool alone. For very sharp fine detail, we hand-carve with tungsten-tipped chisels. There's a wide variety of stonemason's tools on the market for aficionados: pneumatic chisels and grinders and small flexible drive machines that take tiny grinding burrs. Whatever the tools, always remember—safety first! Give yourself plenty of uncluttered space and use protective goggles and a mask.

Stone for carved relief should be of a similar hardness to the pebbles, although you may find granite and quartzite too hard. Marble, in all its lovely colors, might be very tempting but it really is too soft for long-term resistance to acid rain and dirt. In fact, all soft and porous stone should be avoided.

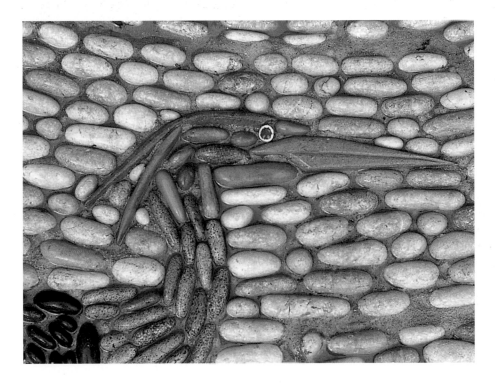

 Grinding a bas-relief detail with a small angle grinder. It can be held in one hand while the other hand manipulates the stone. Work in a comfortable position and use protective goggles and mask. Take extra care if you remove the guard, as I have, in order to get more control.

 A sharp beak and spiky feathers add precision to this heron's head.

 Be patient and take your time when creating a pebble mosaic. Like this detail from a 400-year-old Italian example, a well-executed pebble mosaic should last for centuries.

Take your time

One of the best things about pebble mosaic is its durability: stones are strong, and when a piece is well made it should last for centuries. So why worry about how long it takes to make? Most art takes a disproportionate amount of time and trouble compared to its end use. I have always felt that, when you have a good idea, it should always take "as long as it takes" to realize it.

It may seem crazy and demented to be searching repeatedly for similar tiny stones of a particular shape, or fiddling about trying to blend different colors, or make claws from a few bits of rock. The funny thing is that later, when it's all done, you forget the pain because you're so pleased that it looks good, and other people will be too. They do notice the difference between work that just gets the job done, and work where determination has transformed an ordinary collection of pebbles into a thing of beauty.

2 METHODS FOR IN-SITU PEBBLE MOSAIC

In the last few years, since I made my first suggestions regarding pebble mosaics (in *The Art of Pebble Mosaics*) I've encountered many new in-situ methods. Which method to choose will depend upon the environment, the size of pebbles available, the nature of the traffic using it, and whether or not it should be able to withstand frost. Here I offer some basic advice, together with two methods that are well proven. One is the Mediterranean method shown to me by the Turkish experts, Matusan, who have arrived at a definitive formula for making fine decorative pebble mosaics in a *frost-free* climate. The other is my own method for durable mosaics in a *frost-prone* climate.

IN-SITU METHOD FOR FROST-PRONE AREAS— STEP-BY-STEP

When I returned from an exciting trip to China I made this mosaic (opposite) outside my front door. It was directly inspired by designs I had just seen using a latticework of cut tile sections. It demonstrates the frost-prone climate method.

First, a basic decision: the materials. To achieve a "quiet" look, in keeping with our Lancashire farmhouse, I followed the Chinese dictum: "We use what is available." I collected plain, flat gray river-pebbles locally. I added some of my own spare stock of unevenly shaped white quartz, and purchased some standard 6 in (15 cm) frost-resistant stoneware drainage pipes.

◐ *1 Site preparation. The area is excavated and backfilled with compact aggregate, or crushed stone, 2 in (5 cm) to dust. This is then made level with sand, and then vibrated to form a solid base. The level of the perimeter is established using 4 in x 6 in (10 cm x 15 cm) battens and pegs.*

◐ *2 This is not a straightforward site, but then they seldom are! The drainage gully cannot be moved. The height of the perimeter corresponds to the final top surface. The battens are arranged so that a good fall is achieved towards the gully.*

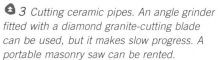 *3 Cutting ceramic pipes. An angle grinder fitted with a diamond granite-cutting blade can be used, but it makes slow progress. A portable masonry saw can be rented.*

4 A dummy run with pipe segments helps to try out various patterns and establish the overall layout.

5 The drainage gully has to be the starting point from which the pipe pattern grows. The segments of pipe are set out across the base and fixed firmly with fillets of mortar.

6 As each line of the pattern is laid out, a long straightedge is used to check the fall over the surface. A 1:50 fall is to be aimed for, so that the pebbles will shed rainwater easily and stay clean. Small gaps are left at the "nodes" of the pattern to allow water to drain from one segment to another.

The dry mix
2 parts sharp $^1/4$ in (5 mm) grit
3 parts sand
1 part cement
Keep it dry. Mix it fresh for each day of work.

▶ *Above left: 7 The lattice of pipe segments is complete and the pebblework begins. A segment is filled with dry mix to approximately ³/4 in (2 cm) below the surface.*

▶ *Above center: 8 Placing pebbles. The longest dimension is placed vertically. The pebbles are touching each other and tightly packed. With these mixed quartz shapes, a random pattern is used.*

▲ *Above right: 9 A stout wooden batten is used to force the pebbles down to a final surface, level with the pipework. A small amount of extra dry-mix is sprinkled onto the pebbles at this stage and brushed in to fill any obvious gaps, but kept well below the top level of the pebbles.*

◀ *10 As each day's work is finished, the area is soaked with clean water from a pressure sprayer. The hardening process of the cement mixture commences immediately and continues for four weeks.*

⬆ *11 The gray flat "skimmer" pebbles are easier to place. Sort the pebbles into "thicks" and "thins" to keep straight rows, and try to offset the joints (as in brickwork) for more strength.*

⬆ *12 The work progresses. It always takes longer than you think it will. We reckoned that this area of pebblework (approximately 135 sq ft [12.5 sq m]) took about 12 full days to complete (not counting the time for site preparation, and the laying of the latticework). It's better not to bite off more than you can chew!*

⬆ *13 A strong edge-support of roughly squared stones. (We could have done this before we started; but, in this case, we wanted to lay out the pattern first and adjust the edge later.)*

◀ *14 Preparing the top mix.*

Top mix

3 parts dry sieved building
  (i.e. soft) sand
1 part *fresh* cement
Measure carefully, in small batches.
Mix thoroughly, then *sieve the mixture again* to ensure a perfectly mixed material.

15 Sufficient top mix is sprinkled on to bring the final surface to approximately $^1/_2$ in (1 cm) below the top of the pebbles. Less or more can be used according to the finished look you want to achieve. In cold wet climates the rapid shedding of water from the surface improves durability, so it's best to use plenty of top mix. Careful brushing with a soft dust-brush produces the final surface.

16 A fine spray is used to soak the top mix. Watch out for the occasional "hole" appearing on the surface (caused by an air pocket). Sprinkle on a little more top mix and spray again.

17 Curing. The mosaic is covered every day during the progress of the pebblework. After the top mix has been applied and sprayed, everything is completely covered for four weeks to ensure maximum strength.

FREQUENTLY ASKED QUESTIONS

Time and again, the same questions are raised by pebble mosaic beginners; so here I'll try to answer a few of them. To illustrate these points, we'll look at a simple project: an "apron" in front of the double doors of Boris's workshop. He wanted something very plain and rural, and we decided on a design that was mostly "plain weave" with colored border patterns to add interest.

How do I prepare the site?

A solid base must be achieved. Depending on the compaction of the site and the type of traffic that might use it, there can be plenty of work to do or very little. Topsoil should always be removed, and the site excavated down to the level of solid subsoil. Then, depending on whether the mosaic is to be subjected to foot-traffic alone, light vehicles or even heavy vehicles (a fire engine perhaps?), the base *beneath* the mosaic must be designed to withstand that type of load. Bases for both in-situ and pre-cast mosaics are the same and are described on page 60.

The edges of the mosaic are particularly vulnerable to damage, and must be well protected. A stout edging of bricks, settings or stone flags should be set on a concrete foundation and haunched. Remember that a heavy-duty specification is necessary for vehicle use. For in-situ work, the edging may be required to serve as the final level for tamping down the pebbles, so it should be carefully set to the right fall so that rainwater is shed from the mosaic surface. If wooden battens are being used to establish the final level and fall, then they are placed in position with pegs or mortar and checked with a spirit-level (see photograph below).

A simple mosaic for Boris's workshop. After excavation, the edging of black granite settings went in first. They were used later as the "guide-level" to which the pebbles will be tamped down, so they had to be carefully placed with their tops at a uniform height to create a "fall" for the finished surface to allow the rainwater to drain away from the door.

Edging level.

How many pebbles do I need?

To calculate the pebbles required, the easiest method is to make a measured trial in sand and *count* the number of pebbles used. Such trials are always useful, not only to calculate number of stones, but to check if you really like the pattern you have in mind. Also, you may find that you haven't enough of the special stones required, in which case you can re-design before you start.

How do I make best use of the pebbles available?

There will always be a lot of variation in the size and the shape of the pebbles. Bought-in ones will have been graded, using a screen of a particular mesh-size; a typical example for in-situ work would be 2–3 in (5–7.5 cm). If you are lucky enough to be able to collect your own, you can aim for uniformity, but you'll need a lot of persistence!

Take time to sort the pebbles thoroughly. Discard any really bad shapes: they are more trouble than they are worth. Keep to one side the "short" ones that you'll need for the ends of rows. Mostly you'll be sorting according to "fatness" so that you can get a uniformity of width for each row. And, as you start another row, use the different lengths of the pebbles to off-set the gaps created in the previous row between the pebbles. Keeping a brickwork-type "bond" both looks good and gives the greatest strength to your work.

Which way up should a pebble be?

Every pebble has a "best" edge. For "long" pebbles this means the longest and flattest. An edge with a protruding point will

⊗ ⊗ *Calculating the number of pebbles needed and sorting them into three piles of thick, medium and thin, to use in different rows.*

- A rough guide when buying pebbles is 25 lb per sq ft or 125 kg per sq m.
- The ratio of pebbles per square meter varies considerably according to the actual size of the pebbles to be used. Larger pebbles equals more weight; smaller pebbles means less.

◄ *To work out the weight and volume of the pebbles required, make a test piece of an exact size, here 20 in (50 cm) square, then dismantle the test and weigh the pebbles. In this instance, using black pebbles between 2–3 in (5 and 7.5 cm) long, 66 lb (30 kg) were used to fill the 2¾ sq ft (¼ sq m) box.*

*Be sure that you have **more than enough pebbles**. You always need a few spare to replace those awkward ones that just won't fit.*

❿ *Use a pointed paint-scraper to dig and loosen the base mix. Then place the pebble and firm the mix around its base.*

❻ ❻ *The base mix should be kept firm: first by treading, and then by pressing it in around the pebbles as you go.*

❻ *Tamp down every row as you go, making sure all the pebbles go down vertically. Note: keeping the previous day's work covered as you go along will prevent drying out and help to keep it clean. It's only too easy to leave a cement stain on the pebbles from the dust on your shoes.*

❻ *As you complete each section, carefully fill gaps with the base mix, bringing it to ¾ in (20–25 mm) below the tops of the pebbles.*

show less surface when the mosaic is finished, and will not look so good.

As you go along, examine each pebble and decide which is the "best" edge for showing on the top surface, bearing in mind the following tips:

- Make sure that it's **deep** enough. A good rule of thumb is that every pebble should be 2 in (5 cm) or more in depth.
- Large long pebbles can often be placed either way, like the one in the picture above left which is deep enough on both sides.
- Try to place the pebbles so they touch the sides of the previous row **and** touch each other end-to-end. The tighter the pebbles are packed together the stronger the mosaic will be.
- A small tool like a pointed paint-scraper will be most useful for digging and loosening the base mix. Dig, place the pebble and then firm the mix around its base.

Why do the pebbles fall over?

When the pebbles are tamped down there is a tendency for the deepest pebbles to lean over because of the resistance of the firmed mix beneath them.

- Remember the "dig, place, firm" routine.
- Place the pebbles so that they stand **only just above** the finished level.
- Tamp down every row, making sure that all the pebbles go down vertically, rather than tipping over. Any tendency to lean over should be corrected immediately.

What about the gaps?

When the section is completed, it's best to make all the pebbles firm by filling up the gaps and bringing the top surface of the base mix to ¾ in (20–25 mm) below the tops of the pebbles. Sprinkle carefully: you don't want to have the gritty particles showing through the final surface of the top mix.

How much water should be used?

Plenty! A soon as you begin to spray the mix with water, the cement begins the chemical reaction which eventually results in hardening, so make sure that the water has penetrated the full depth of the base mix. This first spraying also helps to clean cement dust from the pebbles and wash down any loose particles. Water each day's work as you go along and cover it with polyethylene sheet. The next day it can be walked on and used as a level for adjacent sections if necessary.

How much top mix should be used?

Before you begin with your top mix, remove the polyethylene and make sure that the pebbles are **completely dry**. Then there is a choice to be made:

- the less top mix you use, the better the pebbles will show their shape;
- use more top mix and the surface will be less liable to trap leaves and dirt, and will stay cleaner and easier to sweep.

    My choice here is about ½ in (1.2 cm). Do a small patch at a time. Sprinkle over the surface and brush to perfection. Don't make one central dump and then try to move it out in all directions.

What about the final spraying of the top mix?

No watering cans now! This operation needs care and only a small amount of water. A pressure-sprayer (like a pump-up garden bug-sprayer) will produce a suitable fine jet of mist. Make sure that the sprayer is pumped to a high pressure. Make a test burst on the ground and then spray the mosaic evenly until the surface just floods with water. Then stop. The surface is smoothly bound, and you're done.

⬆ Water each day's work as you go along and cover it with polyethylene sheet. The next day it can be walked on and used as a level for adjacent sections if necessary.

⬅⬅ When your pebble mosaic is finished, sprinkle top mix over the surface, one small patch at a time, and brush into place. Then use a fine mist pressure-sprayer to spray the mosaic evenly so that the surface is smoothly bound.

What about maintenance?

To keep a pebble mosaic clean, sweep it regularly with a stiff yardbrush, or use a garden blower. A gentle annual washing with a cold water power-washer will remove surface dirt, but don't overdo it; the natural weathering of stone is part of the charm of pebble mosaic.

    After many years some deterioration of the top surface may be observed; or a period of neglect may result in some holes and crumbling of the top mix. If the mosaic has been well-made, then restoration is straightforward. Use the cold water power-washer at full power to blast out any loose material and thoroughly clean out the cavities. Then re-dress the surface with fresh top mix, spray and cover to cure. The restored mosaic will be good for another long period of use.

⬆ *A detail from a Matusan design.*

IN-SITU METHOD FOR FROST-FREE AREAS— THE MEDITERRANEAN TECHNIQUE

With thanks to Matusan, who generously share their experience, the process they developed in Turkey is documented here. They make it look easy, but it must be remembered that their expertise was preceded by a long process of experimentation and adjustment. At every stage, meticulous attention is paid to detail.

Points to notice

- The stones are graded to a fairly uniform size: either $1^1/_4$–$1^3/_4$ in (3–4 cm) in length; or 2–$2^1/_2$ in (5–6 cm). They are first-class materials, both hard and smooth. Matusan negotiated special permission for their collection. All gathered by hand from remote southern beaches, carried by donkey, and then graded again by hand in the warehouse, these stones are precious indeed!

- Site preparation is very thorough. A screed of concrete up to 8 in (20 cm) thick is laid in the area which is to take the mosaic. Surrounding paving is all completed before work begins.

- Sometimes a galvanized ($3/_8$ in [8 mm]) or stainless steel ($1/_8$ in [3 mm]) angled-edge support is used instead of a stone surround. This enables lawns or flowerbeds to be brought right up to the edge of the mosaic. Its depth is 4 in (10 cm) to accommodate the pebblework. These supports are tailored into curves and angles by the metal fabricator, who drills into the concrete base and fixes them down with stainless steel screws.

- The mix is placed loosely into the pebble area and lightly leveled off without any compaction, producing a light fluffy texture into which the pebbles are easily pressed. The level of dry mix is set approximately $5/_8$ in (1.5 cm) below the final surface.

- Finishing: the mosaic is completed with a final dusting of *neat dry cement*. This serves to bind the surface and fill any gaps. I was told that the cement "sinks" into the surface when it is flooded with water. It is then lightly brushed and sprayed again.

The mix
2 parts dry sand ($1/_8$ in [3 mm] to dust)
1 part fresh cement

◀ *1* The plywood stencil pattern, ¹/4 in (5 mm) thick, is gently laid in place. Pebblework usually begins with the background. Each pebble is pushed into the dry mix to about one third of its depth, and tightly packed against its neighbors in an upright position. The pebbles stand above the finished level about ¹/2–³/4 in (1.5–2 cm). Note how the pebbles are first placed around the perimeter of each area, and then in rows circulating towards the center. There, a final "eye" stone is carefully selected to fit the gap and make all tight and secure.

◀ *2* Here you see that the stencil has been lifted and placed on the next pattern area. A little adjustment is needed at each join to continue the pattern.

37

3 Pebbles stand $1/2$–$3/4$ in (1.5–2 cm) above the final top surface. They are always placed with their longest dimension vertical. A piece of angled steel helps to support the edge of the work.

4 The contrast color is filled in. Here the blacks are arranged in a herringbone pattern.

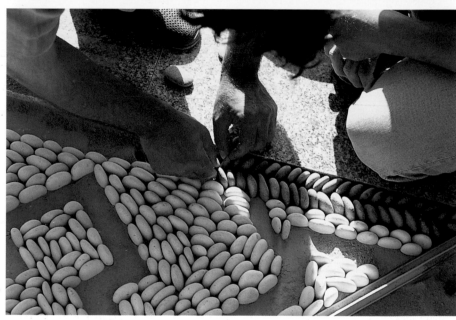

5 A gentle firming to demonstrate the next stage for my benefit. In practice, no real tamping down is done until all the pebbles are in place. Then, the repeated use of the heavy batten forces the pebbles down into the aerated dry mix, while some of the mixture is forced up between the pebbles.

An old method of air-conditioning

In Turkey, and probably throughout the Mediterranean, pebble floors had a practical function as well as an aesthetic one. The burning heat of summer meant that even inside the Ottoman wooden buildings, stone floors warmed up. Outside, they would be too hot for bare feet. To cool the atmosphere, large quantities of water were thrown onto the pebble floors, forming a reservoir in the gaps between the pebbles. The evaporation of water from the hot surface cooled the immediate area and drew in fresh air from outside, creating a moist and cool microclimate.

This aspect of the pebble mosaics of the past (their function as not only an aesthetic but also a physical luxury) had completely escaped me until the mosaicists of Matusan pointed it out. It explains why Mediterranean pebble mosaics have a close-packed uniform texture and deep gaps between the pebbles. The gaps hold the water, which acts as the coolant. It reminds me of the way Indian princes constructed pavilions with outdoor thrones placed directly over the cooling waters of the mihrab (a textured stone ramp over which water trickled). And those channels of flowing water cascading down either side of the staircase at the Generalife in the Alhambra in Granada; and the grand water cascades and grottoes of the Italian renaissance; they were not just conceived as a beautiful landscape and architectural concept, but to create relief from the fierce heat of the day.

⬆ *The Wray mosaic was made as a community project to celebrate the millennium. The plywood stencils were tacked onto 4 in (10 cm) blocks to create simple formers. Stones were gathered from the river and laid in lines of increasing width to emphasize the "flow." Later, the stencils were lifted out and the gaps filled with white pebbles.*

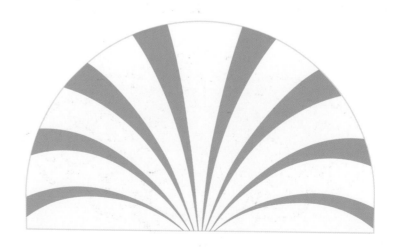

The "Flood" mosaic at Wray, U.K. The fan shapes, representing the gush of floodwater that occurred in 1969, were made using large stencils. The patterns were generated on a computer from a tracing of the original design (see opposite). A simple alternative would be to draw a grid onto the original scale drawing, and scale up to actual size by hand. The resulting paper patterns are transferred to plywood and cut out with a handheld electric jigsaw.

A Matusan design which will be transferred to plywood at actual size to form a number of stencils for making the mosaic.

DIVIDING UP A LARGE AREA

For large areas, some form of subdivision must be made so that the pebbles can be tamped down section by section. Usually long wooden battens are used for this, 4 in x 2 in (10 cm x 5 cm), secured with pegs, and wedged to the correct height. They are so placed to delineate the main areas of the design, e.g., the border, the center and each quarter. The pebblework will be tamped down to the level of the battens, so make the strips or segments approximately 40 in (1 m) apart. The way the area is divided is governed by the design; with a completely free-flowing design, the divisions will be arbitrary.

⬆ Long stout battens are held in place with steel pegs hammered into the base, then wedged firmly to the correct height with thin slates or tiles. Here, a bank has been divided into a border section at the top and several sloping sections below. Diamond shapes were made, using a removable mold fastened with string. As the first batch was completed, the molds were removed and reassembled to complete the alternate patterns. Gosforth, Cumbria, U.K.

⬆ The proud finish of the Gosforth village mosaic. There's no doubt that many hands made light work! An enthusiastic group made this 200 sq ft (18 sq m) mosaic in five days of hard work. Many commented that it reminded them of "old times"—working together in a hands-on activity to make a permanent improvement to their village.

◀◀ In-situ project at Watchet, Devon, U.K. Long battens are laid in place to divide the area, wedged to the correct height to maintain the fall from the center to the drainage points. Here a stencil has been used to create the wave pattern.

◀◀ A cautionary tale! Making in-situ mosaics requires thorough, painstaking work. This sorry picture, taken on Rhodes, shows what can happen.

3 PRECAST TECHNIQUE FOR PEBBLE MOSAIC

There are many reasons why the in-situ making technique is not always appropriate: time and distance, availability of material, size of final mosaic and, not least, the weather. In these circumstances, a workshop production technique is required in which the pebble mosaic is precast in one place, and then transported to its final destination and installed.

The technique has several advantages:

- *Durability*: The strength of a precast slab, using nonshrink grout and wet-mixed concrete, is far superior to a dry-mix technique.
- *Comfort*: All your work can be done on a bench, under cover. Come rain or freeze, you are unaffected.
- *Unlimited time*: If you feel like making complex designs and taking a couple of days to make a single piece, there's no problem with either aching knees or setting concrete.
- *Ability to use smaller pebbles*: The nonshrink grout used in the first stage of the casting process is very strong. It's designed for pouring into the foundations of steel-framed buildings, so in the unlikely and unfortunate event of you actually managing to break a mosaic slab, you'll find that it breaks *across the pebbles* rather than along the lines of the grout. This amazing strength means that it is possible to use quite tiny pebbles for your mosaic, as small as you can conveniently manipulate by hand (even with tweezers, if you have the inclination).
- *Flat surface*: Since the sections of the mosaic are created upside down, they will have an absolutely flat surface.

However, this is not an easy technique, and certainly not one for beginners. Practice making in-situ mosaics first before trying precast. This will help to train your eye in selecting pebbles for width, depth and length, and choosing the best way up for each pebble. When you get used to selecting pebbles for their "right way up," turning them about to find their best upper surface, then you'll be ready for the precast process of turning them upside down.

Working upside down is rather like working "blind." Placing the pebbles is an act of faith: you just don't know what it's going to look like. It may take days in the making, and then it has to be cast; and it's not until the day after, when you turn it over, that you get to see it. This is normally an exciting and pleasurable moment, provided all has gone well.

A good rule
Each slab should measure no more than about 6 sq ft ($1/2$ sq m) in area.

THE PRECAST METHOD STEP BY STEP: A SMALL PRECAST SUN MOSAIC IN THE GARDEN.

▶ 1. The design

Having decided upon the sun as the motif, the first step is to consider the practicalities: the size and weight. This one is 30 in (75 cm) square. That's about 6 sq ft (¹/₂ sq m) in area. At 3 in (7.5 cm) thick, it will weigh 100 lb (45 kg). Think of this as a maximum. Of course, you can make bigger slabs, but your back will suffer when you have to move them. Remember that each slab must be turned after casting, then moved for storage, and eventually lifted into its final position. Slabs should be no heavier than two people can easily handle.

 2. The pattern
The design is drawn on paper and placed on a baseboard of 3/4 in (2 cm) blockboard, or similar, on the bench. A protective layer of polyethylene is taped down over it.

 3. Assembling the mold
Wooden battens 3 1/2 in x 2 in (9 cm x 5 cm) are assembled over the pattern and nailed down. Pre-drill the battens with holes of a slightly larger diameter than the nails you will be using to hold the battens firmly onto the base.

 5. Putting in the pebbles upside down
Each pebble has to be selected for size and shape and placed with its eventual top surface upside down. With experience, this will become automatic: a quick glance to find each pebble's best aspect, then down it goes, closely packed alongside its neighbor. The border stones near the sides of the mold are easy to place, but in the center the pebbles have an irritating habit of falling over until the whole patch is done and they all hold each other upright. Here, small blocks of stone are being used as extra props to start with.

Patience

It requires patient practice to get the "rebate" even. No one gets it right the first time. Getting it wrong gives a horrible result: pebbles projecting from a blobby background, occasionally covered with extraneous grout where it has penetrated around and beneath the pebbles in the mold.

 4. Organizing the pebbles
You will find that far more pebbles are needed than you can possibly imagine. Assemble and sort plenty of them ready for action. Here, for the eyes, nose and mouth of the sun's face, we have tried out the arrangement "dry." The eyes are two banded pebbles, as nearly matching as we could find; there's a special wedge-shaped stone for the nose; and the mouth is a slice of frost-proof ceramic drainpipe.

⬆ 6. Using the sand
As each pebble is placed in the mold, dry sieved sand is worked around it to a depth of 5/16 in (8 mm). When the mosaic is eventually cast, this sand will be washed away, leaving each pebble pleasingly projecting as though pushing up through the grout. I call this the "rebate." This is the difficult bit: mastering the skill of getting an even depth of sand. The pebbles should just touch each other, with the sand evenly distributed in the gaps. You are doing three things simultaneously: placing your pebble, following the base pattern and brushing the sand around it. Practice makes perfect!

⬆ 7. Testing the sand depth
Here's a useful tool to test the depth of the sand. Use a Stanley knife to whittle the end of a stick (the type of split bamboo stick used for supporting houseplants is good). Whittle it to a narrow peg 5/16 in (8 mm) in length, which is the chosen sand-depth. This could be adjusted to a greater depth for larger stones or lesser for tiny ones. Use the stick as you go along, to check that you are getting the depth right. When you poke the stick into the sand it should just touch the top of the peg.

A note on depth
A slab of up to 6 sq ft (1/2 sq m) can be 3 in (7.5 cm) deep, but if you want to use any large stones, then about 31/2 in (9 cm) is better.

⬖ 8. A final check
Only a very few people manage to acquire the skill to get the sand depth accurate every time. I'm not one of them, so I have to invent these tricks. Here's another. Fill a cutoff dishwashing liquid bottle with dry sand and use it to dribble tiny quantities of sand into the mold where needed: sand-depth stick in one hand, sand bottle in the other, with index finger acting as the stopper. Provided that you had the sand depth nearly right as the pebbles went in, this checking over should correct any little discrepancies. The worst mistake is to get too much sand in the mold. Result: pebbles standing out like sore thumbs or uncomfortable beds of nails.

9. Wetting the sand

First, wet the sand thoroughly with a fine pressure sprayer. If you forget to do this, the dry sand will suck the water from the grout and you risk getting air pockets and uneven penetration of grout between the pebbles.

10. Mixing the grout

A specialized cementitious grout should be used. It is shrinkage-compensated. There are several brands to be found in larger building supply stores in major towns and cities. It comes ready-prepared for use: all you do is add the correct amount of water (usually 5 quarts to a 56 lb bag [5 liters to 25 kg]) and mix thoroughly. Use a paddle attachment on an electric drill for thorough mixing; it will eliminate lumps with ease.

It is expensive, but the importance of using this special grout cannot be overemphasized: It has a flowing property which enables the grout to penetrate through the little gaps between the pebbles (which are, of course, tightly packed). It is enormously strong. Most important, it will not shrink away from the pebbles. Ordinary mortar mixed with so large a proportion of water will shrink hopelessly: in five years your pebbles will be popping out.

11. Pouring the grout

A gentle hammering on the base helps to make sure that there are no air bubbles trapped between the pebbles and makes the grout spread out evenly.

Now the mosaic must be left for a while for the grout to stiffen to the consistency of putty. The time (one to six hours) will vary according to the air temperature. The grout should partially set so that the pebbles are held firmly but the grout remains plastic. It will then hold your pebblework safely in the next stage, which involves vigorous tamping and vibrating. But don't let the grout get too hard or you risk cracks on the surface.

Golden rule

At least two-thirds of each pebble must be embedded. So watch out for those small rounded ones, and for pebbles which appear to fit beautifully, but are really not big enough to bed deeply below the rebate.

⬆ 12. Filling the mold
The mold is filled with concrete. Take special care to work the mixture down at the edges. Avoid knocking any pebbles that protrude above the grout. The concrete should completely fill the mold.

⬆ 13. Tamping the concrete
The best way to consolidate the concrete in the mold is to use a stout piece of timber as a tamping bar. Resting on the sides and the brimming concrete, tamp back and forth, adding a little more mix here and there until a homogenous smooth surface is achieved. You can "strike off" excess mix by "sawing" in a sideways action if necessary. Even better consolidation of the concrete can be achieved if you have a vibrating table. Use it at its lowest setting for a minimum length of time in which to expel air bubbles. Don't be tempted to overdo it, or you risk disturbing the pebbles.

When the casting is complete, cover the mold with polyethylene and seal the edges to prevent drying out. The concrete will "go off" in a short while, and will attain a state of reasonable hardness by the following day.

⬆ 14. Turning out the mosaic
The grout and concrete are still "green" by the next day, so you need to be careful not to knock the edges off when turning the mosaic over. Now comes the exciting moment: you brush off the sand to reveal the mosaic (the first time you will have seen it!) A thorough hosing down removes the last bit of damp sand.

The concrete mix
3 parts same-size ³/₈ in (1 cm) aggregate
2 parts concreting sand
1 part fresh cement
For strength, use as little water as possible to attain a workable consistency. A concrete plasticizer is recommended.

⬆ 15. Any corrections
While the grout and concrete are "green," this is an opportunity to chisel off any little bits of grout that are in the wrong place. The edges of the mosaic are often sharp and can be easily rounded off at this stage.

⬆ 16. Curing
The mosaic should be completely enclosed in polyethylene and the edges sealed to prevent it drying out during the curing of the concrete. Initial curing takes three days, during which it acquires 90 percent of its strength. Maximum strength is only reached after 28 days. For all of this time the mosaic must be kept damp and enclosed in polyethylene wraps.

SOME PRECAST MOSAIC PROJECTS

Tugnet sculpture project

◀◀ ▲ ◀ The Tugnet sculpture project is a series of pebble mosaics made for the Icehouse Visitor Centre at Spey Bay, Morayshire, U.K. Scenes from local life, history and wildlife are shown in a series of mosaics set into the grass. Inspiration must have come from the huge banks of pebbles found on the shore of the Moray coast: a beautiful range of colored granites and quartzes. Children and teachers from Milne High School drew the designs and made the panels. They decided to simplify the mold-making by cutting the designs into 24 in (60 cm) squares for ease of working. Although the joins are noticeable, they are surprisingly inoffensive because great care has been taken to maintain continuity from panel to panel, and the overall texture of the pebblework is small and uniform.

◀ A delightful precast mosaic by Janette Ireland. A single piece like this, only 24 in x 15 in (60 cm x 37.5 cm) makes a garden feature that acts as a "welcome mat," and enhances this threshold with a pleasant textural panel, like a stitched sampler. Even-sized pebbles suggest these kinds of patterns: herringbone, cross-stitch and French knots.

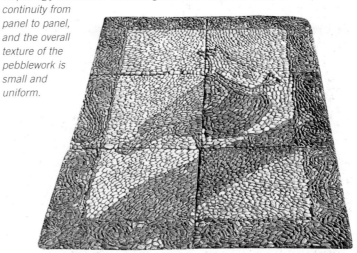

Alderney millennium mosaic project

The millennium galvanized many communities into action. The small population of the Channel Island of Alderney, U.K., was enthusiastic about a permanent feature on the island, and wanted to make it themselves. An astonishing number of different groups were drawn into the project: 20 organizations made mosaics under the direction of a central mosaic committee. The simplicity of these mosaics belies the enormous amount of community effort involved: the willingness to learn a difficult technique, cooperation in design-making, co-ordination of group activities and, finally, bringing all the mosaics into a permanent setting.

⬆ *A portrait of the Alderney cow, a special breed peculiar to the island.*

⏩ *The mosaics, each one 24 in (60 cm) square and made by a different group, were set into the churchyard path in St. Peter Port. It makes an interesting walk for everyone, and carries great meaning for the island community. The quiet colors of the pebbles and the pathway harmonize with the traditional rural surroundings.*

⏩ *At the start of the path an open book announces the Millennium Mosaic.*

The centerpiece of the Melling mosaic is this stylized tractor wheel with a rainbow background: two ideas combined. It makes an effective focal point in the semicircle and centers on the doorway into the institute.

A charming owl made with mixed shades of red and brown pebbles. The typical owl face is emphasized by making the pebbles circulate around the eyes (a single black flint split in two).

Melling millennium mosaic project

Opening ceremony for the Melling mosaic, U.K., placed at the entrance to the village institute. Many of the people in this photograph made sections of the mosaic, and all helped. The design process was a communal activity: everyone produced sketches of aspects of village life. My function, at this point, was to weld all these different images into a unified and pleasing design. Here, the computer was a godsend! I scanned each drawing, scaled it, and arranged each one within the overall agreed ground plan. This was semicircular in shape with a central tractor wheel motif (symbolizing the farming community) and a wavy border (our river). Although, in this case, the mold-making was simplified as much as possible, there were some complicated shapes to construct. For more on drafting patterns with the computer see chapter 4.

A design for a mosaic 6 ft 7 in (2 m) in diameter.

LARGER PRECAST MOSAICS—MAKING IT ALL FIT TOGETHER

One-piece mosaics are inevitably limited to a size that can be handled comfortably. Even four strong men balk at anything over 10 or 11 sq ft (1 sq m). Larger mosaics must be split into manageable sections. Each section must be tailored to fit together with its neighbors exactly, allowing a small margin for "ease."

A design with many straight lines is straightforward because the cuts between sections will follow the main outlines, and straight wooden battens can be used for assembling the molds. However, the task gets more complicated when the sections have curved outlines.

Making molds with curvy jigsawlike shapes

Sometimes a mold made up of straight lines just does not suit the design. Many of the images which are so appropriate for pebblework (flowers, animals, waves) are made with flowing curving lines, so they must be treated in a different way. It looks wrong to cut across a curved image with an arbitrary straight line; the "cut" should follow the form. I believe that it's well worth the trouble to work with these lines of flow so that the joints are barely noticeable. Where a cut has to be made across an open area (of background, for instance) it will appear as a decorative latticework, similar to the tracery of a stained-glass window.

A woodworker with access to a band saw will have no problems cutting out particular shapes for the walls of molds. Although expensive in time and materials, employing a specialized woodworker becomes economical when the molds are to be used many times, in a repeat border, for instance. Sealed with varnish, and carefully cleaned after each use, a wooden mold can be used for

The cuts are drawn with a fat marker (tip about 3/8 in [1 cm]) onto a hand-drawn pattern; or, using a computer, drawn to the proportional line-width for later scaling up. Note the reversed image for the patterns. The cuts follow the curves of the design, chopping the mosaic into portions of a suitable size.

⊕ *The finished mosaic, assembled "dry" before installation. The joints are very inconspicuous.*

Important points

- Make an accurate pattern with the "cuts" or joints clearly marked; 5/32 in (7 mm) is an average width for each joint.
- Assemble molds accurately to the joint lines of the pattern.
- Check that the sides of the mold are exactly 90°.

◗ *A temporary mold made with blocks* The mosaic pattern is placed on the baseboard and protected with transparent polyethylene, which is taped to the base for protection. Then the various blocks are chosen to follow the curves and peculiarities of the mold. Accuracy is important, otherwise the mosaic will not fit well, and the joints will be wider and more noticeable. Strips of stiff plastic are used to line the walls of the mold. These protect the blocks and span the small gaps between them. They are taped to the tops of the blocks and the base of the mold. It is all very temporary and simple in concept; but it is strong enough to withstand the pressures of the casting process. Afterwards it can all be stripped away, cleaned and recycled.

a hundred casts. If it is to be used many more times, it could be worth investing in the type of fiberglass and rubber molds used by the concrete industry.

More commonly though, each mold will be used once only, and for this there must be a different approach. In my workshop we use small wooden blocks, resembling children's play bricks, in a variety of shapes: square, triangular, with 45° and 20° angles, and some with curved edges of different radii. We also use many sections cut from PVC pipes ranging from 2 in (5 cm) radius to 24 in (60 cm).

All are cut to the chosen depth for the mosaic mold. The wooden blocks are each pre-drilled with two holes, through which long nails are hammered into the baseboard.

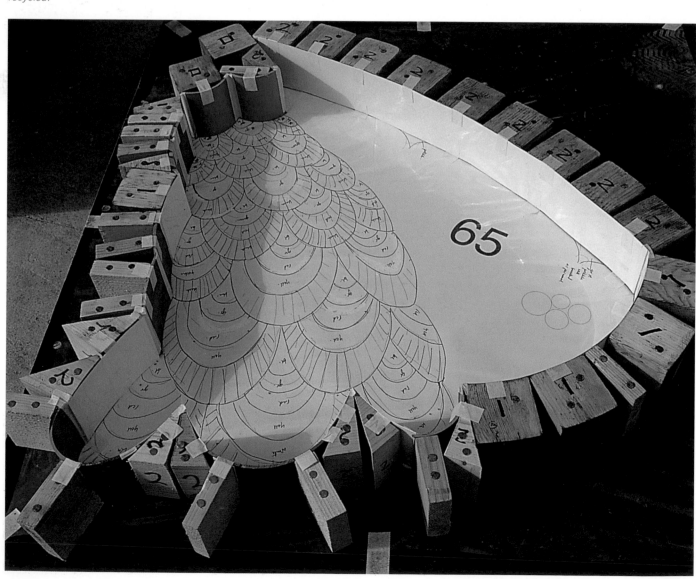

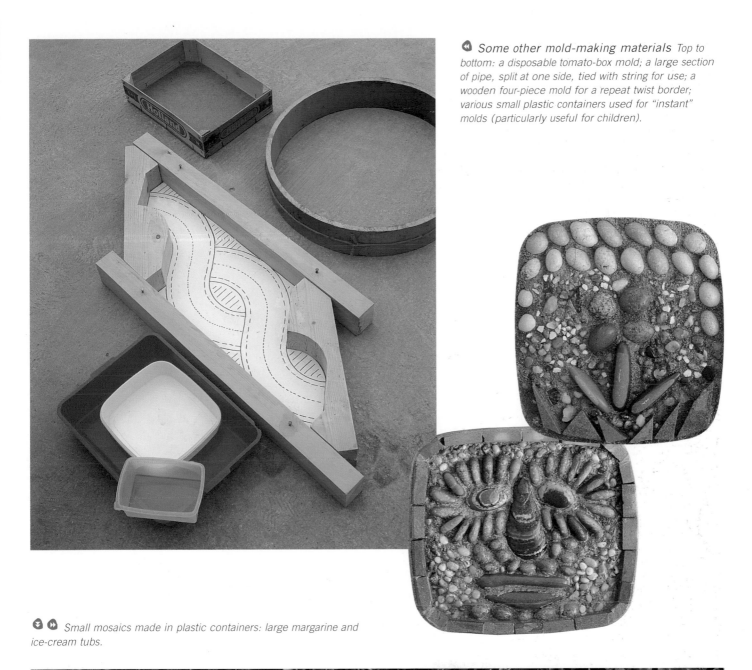

◀ *Some other mold-making materials* Top to bottom: *a disposable tomato-box mold; a large section of pipe, split at one side, tied with string for use; a wooden four-piece mold for a repeat twist border; various small plastic containers used for "instant" molds (particularly useful for children).*

◑ ◐ *Small mosaics made in plastic containers: large margarine and ice-cream tubs.*

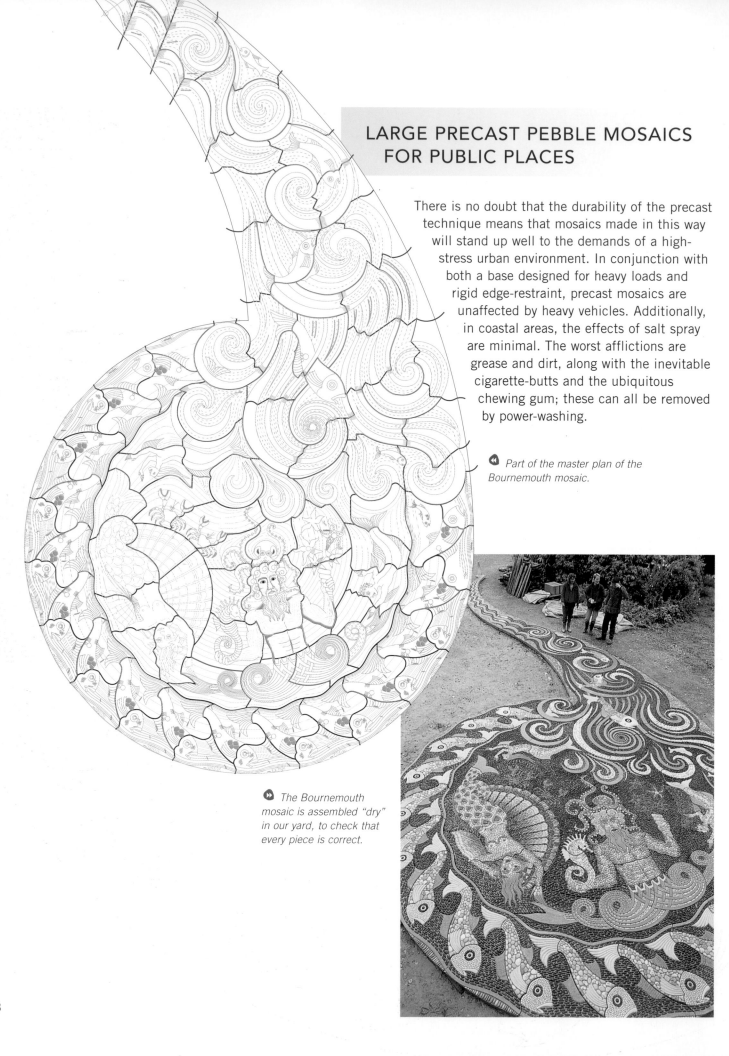

LARGE PRECAST PEBBLE MOSAICS FOR PUBLIC PLACES

There is no doubt that the durability of the precast technique means that mosaics made in this way will stand up well to the demands of a high-stress urban environment. In conjunction with both a base designed for heavy loads and rigid edge-restraint, precast mosaics are unaffected by heavy vehicles. Additionally, in coastal areas, the effects of salt spray are minimal. The worst afflictions are grease and dirt, along with the inevitable cigarette-butts and the ubiquitous chewing gum; these can all be removed by power-washing.

◂ *Part of the master plan of the Bournemouth mosaic.*

▸ *The Bournemouth mosaic is assembled "dry" in our yard, to check that every piece is correct.*

This large mosaic, weighing eight tons, was made in over a hundred sections. It took just a week to install. Despite its size, it appears quite small in the context of this vast square in Bournemouth, U.K.

INSTALLING PRECAST MOSAICS

Requirements:
- a site plan with all the pieces numbered
- strong people to lift and place the slabs
- strong straps for awkwardly fitting pieces
- a long level
- a long straightedge
- dry weather

There are many opinions among building contractors as to the best way to lay slabs. Some prefer to use a dry mix of sharp or concreting sand and cement, packing each slab individually as they go along. Some like to set the slabs on "dabs" of wet mortar, which they spread under each slab and tap down to the correct level. Either of these methods is OK for pedestrian use only, but not for vehicle use.

The method I prefer is this: a continuous bed of pliable mortar, which is spread on the concrete base. As each slab is laid, the level is adjusted by tapping with a large rubber mallet. Using this method, the slabs are "solid bedded." Provided that the base beneath has been designed for the loading intended, there should be no possibility of damage. This method is essential for heavy traffic situations.

Bases for precast pebble mosaics

Single pieces and small mosaics in gardens: pedestrian use only	Can be bedded on sand over compact aggregate base. Mosaics with several pieces will be easier to lay on a minimal layer of concrete.
Drives, paths, light vehicle use	A minimum base layer of 6 in (15 cm) of compact aggregate or coarse granular stone, well compacted, plus 4 in (10 cm) of 1:2:3 concrete.
Heavy vehicle use	Concrete base 8–12 in (20–30 cm) with steel reinforcement and rigid edge-restraint. A structural engineer should advise for each specific application.

THE FALL

Any pebble mosaic, whether precast or in-situ construction, will benefit from a good "fall" over the surface. A good average to aim for is 1:50; 1:66 is, I believe, a minimum. The "fall" allows rainwater to drain away by gravity: this helps both to keep the mosaic clean and to counteract the retentive effect of any little imperfections in the rebate surface. It should be established before installation, when the concrete base is laid. This means that when the slabs come to be laid on top, all attention can be given to spreading an even depth of mortar for each slab, and leveling each one to the next.

For large mosaics, it may be necessary to "crown" the mosaic, or to create a "ridge" or a "dish," casting the rainwater to the perimeter or to a central gully. This requirement adds a slight three-dimensional complication to the laying of the slabs. Take it into account at the design stage by arranging the "cuts" in the mosaic to coincide with the direction of the "fall," thus avoiding awkward diagonal pieces spanning a ridge or valley.

◑ *This large mosaic at Lytham, U.K., was "crowned" in order to cast rainwater to the perimeter. The central slab was laid first, at the correct height; and then, working from the center, a long straightedge of lumber was used constantly to maintain an even fall over the surface. Two hundred sections were laid, attracting quite a crowd.*

GROUTING THE JOINTS IN THE MOSAIC

1. Take your time! Choose a dry day without wind. You'll need clean water and a bathroom sponge to mop up spills, and rubber gloves to protect your hands.
2. Dampen the joints with water from a spray. This helps the grout to flow along the joints and integrate smoothly with the top surface.
3. Mix the grout in a bucket really thoroughly. Don't be tempted to make larger quantities. Use a mixer paddle attached to an electric drill. There must not be any lumps. Proportions are normally about 1 quart of water to 11 lb (1 L to 5 kg) of grout, so find a container to measure small quantities. The consistency should be that of thick pouring cream. A little more water can be added if the joints are very tight.
4. The job is best accomplished in two stages. First, fill the joints to within 1/2 in (1.5 cm) of the surface. This is best achieved using a small domestic measuring jug with a good lip. Don't fill it more than half full.

❂ Using the same non-shrink pourable grout as is used in the casting process, the joints in the mosaic are filled.

◀ *This is like "invisible mending." The final drops of grout are poured to fill the joints in the mosaic. With care, it is possible to make the joints quite inconspicuous. To the right of the picture, you can see the dry sand which has been sprinkled on while the grout is still wet to make it match the surface of the cast blocks.*

The grout flows along the joints, so pour as accurately as possible into the joints at any convenient point, and mop up any spills as you go. A short pause will allow any sinking to take place.

5   Now for the second stage. A good final appearance requires that great care is taken at this point. In general, it will look best if you can *slightly* overfill the joints. But you must avoid creating a ridge and giving the joint a "welded" look. If you keep the surface damp, the excess grout will *just* flow over the surrounding previously cast surface of the mosaic. With the sponge, clean off any grout on the pebbles. It will look much worse later when it's dry, and will be very hard to remove then.

6   While the grout is *still wet* it must be sprinkled with dry sieved sand (the same used in fabrication of the mosaic). Do it section by section as you go along.

7   While the grout is soft it must be protected from rain. Whatever the weather, it's best to cover the mosaic completely with polyethylene for several days.

4 USING THE COMPUTER TO MAKE PATTERNS FOR PEBBLE MOSAIC: A BRIEF INTRODUCTION FOR BEGINNERS

Experienced computer users may well wish to skip this section; it is intended only as a primer for those mosaicists who would like to make large mosaics by the precast method and have not yet figured out how useful a computer can be with this job. It will, I hope, help those of you who are as bewildered by computers and their programs as I was, when I began.

I decided to learn how to use a computer when I became dissatisfied with the time taken to draft the patterns for the mosaic. This stage always requires taking the scale drawing of the design and enlarging it to full size: a process that used to involve crawling over a large sheet of paper on the floor and scaling everything up to size by hand. It was backbreaking and messy, and I knew that a computer would be the answer to the problem. But there was no one to advise me, and it was a long, hard learning-curve, particularly as I had never used a computer before. Here are a few hints I picked up on the way.

DON'T EXPECT THE COMPUTER TO THINK FOR YOU

Remember that the computer is only a tool; it cannot give you inspiration or ideas for designs, or solve the physical problems of suitable stones for making individual pebble mosaics. It cannot make your original sketches for you. I have always found it hopeless to draw creatively on a computer screen. It's far quicker and easier to draw by hand first, and then to trace the design using a scanner and suitable program.

I bought my first computer expecting that the jobs I wanted it to perform would be very simple. I thought I'd be able to scan my hand-drawn designs onto it, scale them up, then print them out—bingo! But I soon encountered a problem: I discovered that I had to magnify my little drawing about 10 times to get anything remotely big enough to use for pebblework. Then, not only did the original lines come out looking fat and fuzzy, but many of the details were unsatisfactory. A bird's beak drawn at 1:10 might look fine but, blown up 10 times, it needs a bit more care and precision. So, although it's tempting to simply use the computer to enlarge your images to a size suitable for pebblework, you will find this way of working useful only occasionally.

VECTOR GRAPHICS

This sounds fearsome, but it's only a computer tool. Take your time and learn to master it, and you will find that you can draw all your details precisely, rather than expecting to improvise as you go along.

Vector graphics is a clever invention whereby the computer records visual information in dots, which are defined by mathematical coordinates. Each dot is joined to the next by lines or curves. When you have broken your drawing down to these elements, the program has a set of tools available that makes it possible to alter the drawing in any way. Once you've learned this art of manipulation, you will be able to redraw your original with much greater precision, making the most beautiful curves (even better than you could by hand). Having reworked your drawing to perfection, you will be able to stretch it, scale it, color it, write on it and eventually print it, all with ease.

PROGRAMS

The programs I use are Illustrator and Photoshop, both contained in Adobe Creative Suite. Using a scanner, Photoshop will copy your original drawing (as a bit-mapped image) for subsequent tracing in Illustrator (as vectors). Adobe are continually updating these applications with more sophisticated tools to make your job easier (an example is Live Trace in CS2), so the following pages outline very simply the steps you must take to achieve workshop-ready patterns.

◀◀ An original design in pencil, drawn at 1:10 scale. All the creative thinking is here: the drawing attempts to convey the texture of the pebbles and the context of the mosaic, which is a country park in a natural setting of stream and woodland. Once the decision is taken to proceed, this original design must be transformed into patterns that can be used for construction of the mosaic.

THE BASIC PROCEDURE FOR DRAFTING MOSAIC PATTERNS ON THE COMPUTER

1 Scan the drawing in Photoshop (200 ppi will do) and save.

2 Open Illustrator (or other vector program) and open the image as a background layer. Adapt the scale of the original if necessary. Now trace with the drawing tools. Use different layers for the main drawing, the colors, the pebble direction, the external perimeter and anything else that is convenient. This is your master drawing.

3 Don't forget to *mirror the whole design* for the precast upside-down technique.

4 Scale the whole thing up to a thousand percent (10 times the original size). Keep line widths the same, or adjust to suit. Large mosaics will probably be done in two stages. The drawing area on my computer is about 10 ft (3 m) maximum, so for a mosaic larger than this, I scale up 250 percent at this stage and 400 percent later, when I've created each piece of the mosaic as a separate document.

5 Draw the "cuts" or joints between the sections of the mosaic. I use a line 1/4 in (6 mm) wide (sometimes 3/16 in [5 mm]). It's easier to do an accurate job at this stage, after scaling. I use a store of saved curves that correspond to the sections of curved lumber and pipe I use for constructing the molds. Using these curves on the master drawing makes for more accuracy in mold-making, and better fitting of the mosaic sections. Remember to keep the size of each mosaic slab *manageable*. Too big means too heavy, and that means injured backs. As a general rule the

❤ *A tracing of the essential lines of the original design. The clearer the better; pen and ink or a clean pencil drawing*

slab should be no more than 3 ft 4 in (1 m) in any direction (an average size of 24 in x 24 in [60 cm x 60 cm] will be fine).

6 The text instructions (color, type and size of pebbles) and slab numbers are best put in at this stage, after scaling. Remember that text increases the file size enormously and can make the master document unwieldy. This completes your final master. Save a copy in case anything goes haywire.

7 Each piece of the mosaic has to be "cut out" of the master drawing and copied into a separate document. Use the direct selection tool to select all the information for each numbered piece; make a copy, and then cut away all extraneous lines with the scissors tool. **Take care**. It's easy to move a line slightly without noticing, or to leave a few lines out. Any final scaling gets done now, and a page size is selected for each piece.

8 Print them all out. Large-format printers are remarkably accurate. A

⬆ All the drawing is complete. It has been flipped over to make a mirror image; the joints in the mosaic have been marked and the sections numbered.

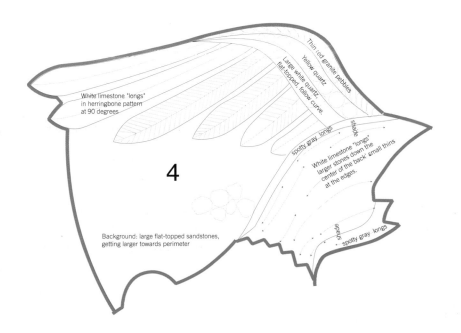

◀◀ A pattern piece.

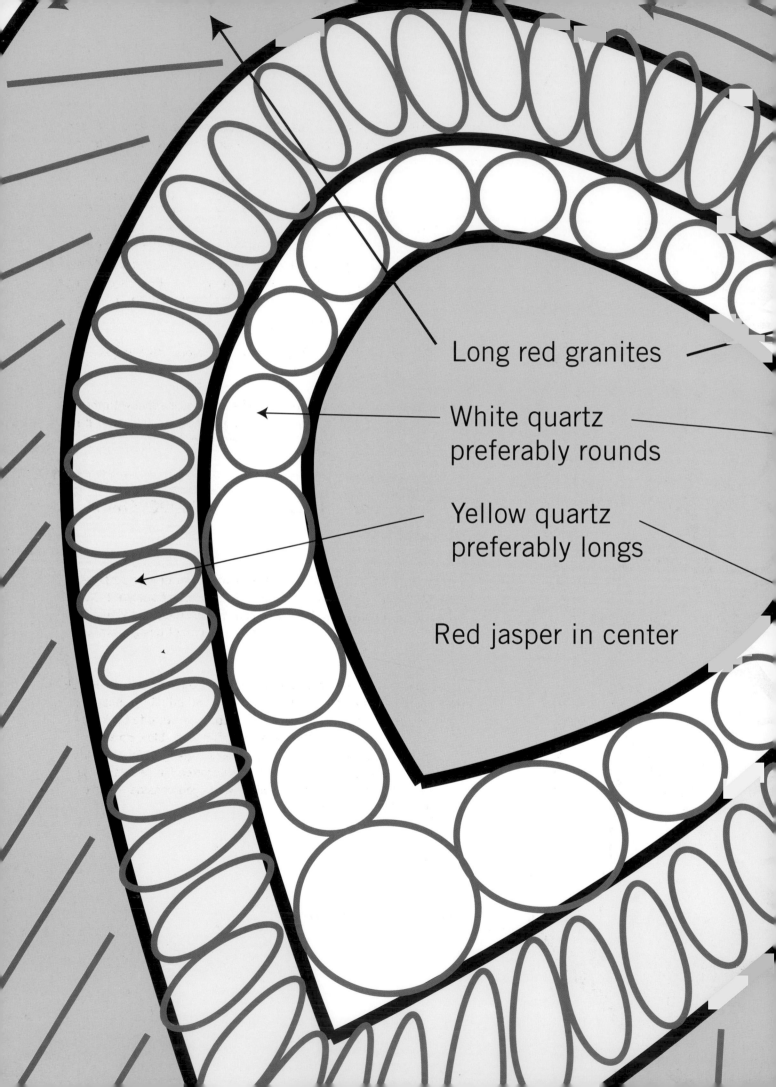

Long red granites

White quartz
preferably rounds

Yellow quartz
preferably longs

Red jasper in center

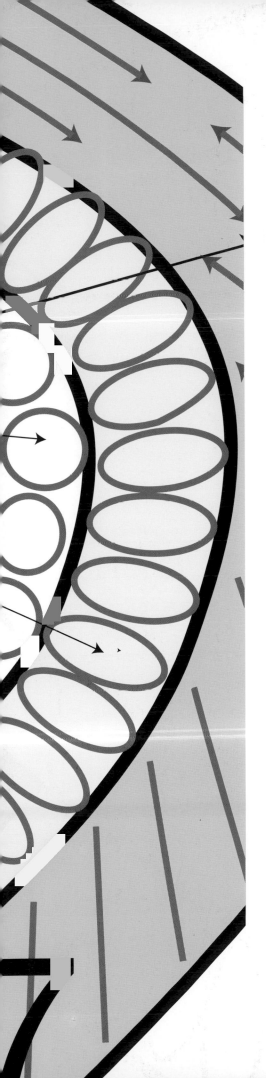

very slight amount of "stretch" can be observed on long pieces of paper, but it's of no consequence compared to the possible inaccuracies of the mold-making.

I use a coated medium-weight bond paper (90 gsm). It's cheap enough, and makes nicer prints than plain paper. My printer works up to 36 in wide (90 cm) and up to 9 ft long (2.7 m); plenty big enough for mosaic patterns (most will be approximately 33 in by 47 in, or A0 size, some 33 in by 23 1/2 in, or A1 size). Although full color is nice, it's expensive on ink cartridges. So I tend to reduce tones to a pastel shade and use color only when I need to clarify something on the design (maybe for shading). When I want a full-color print to show to a client, or for a site plan, I can beef up the color again.

9   Print out the master plan too. Of course, it is a reverse plan and is helpful for sorting out the patterns.

10 Print out a site plan, as well. Flip the whole thing over again with the mirror tool. Leave out the text, but adjust the numbers. You'll need this to assemble the finished mosaic without confusion.

OTHER USEFUL THINGS YOU CAN DO ON A COMPUTER

- Scan in bits of designs that you like, and adapt them to your purposes. Design sourcebooks can be useful, especially those that analyze historic styles and museum artifacts. Illustrations of jewelry, stone carvings, manuscript illumination, heraldry, ceramics and carpet designs are all valuable sources for ideas.

- Photographs of actual subjects such as birds and animals can be useful. After all, you don't often get a wild animal to stand still long enough in an interesting pose for you to draw it. Illustrations in wildlife books are helpful in showing characteristic poses. But, simply to blow up an illustration and use it as a pattern for a mosaic is going to result in a very wooden-looking mosaic. The form must be *interpreted* in pebbles. Use the illustration as a basis for your drawing, while you consider pebble sizes and the flow of the pattern.

◂◂ *Part of an actual-size pattern for pebble mosaic.*

USEFUL COMPUTER DRAWING TOOLS

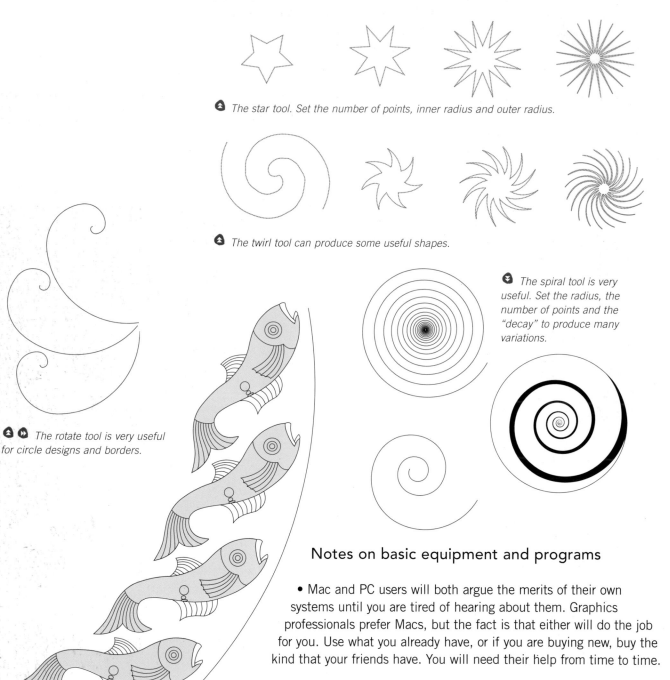

The star tool. Set the number of points, inner radius and outer radius.

The twirl tool can produce some useful shapes.

The spiral tool is very useful. Set the radius, the number of points and the "decay" to produce many variations.

The rotate tool is very useful for circle designs and borders.

Notes on basic equipment and programs

• Mac and PC users will both argue the merits of their own systems until you are tired of hearing about them. Graphics professionals prefer Macs, but the fact is that either will do the job for you. Use what you already have, or if you are buying new, buy the kind that your friends have. You will need their help from time to time.

• Buy only what you really need at the time. A big monitor is a nice luxury: you will be able to see your designs much better. A fast graphics card is essential (not a games card), and plenty of memory is worthwhile.

• Remember that you can often get "free" programs already installed when you buy good new equipment.

- Adobe programs for graphics are excellent, and available for Macs or PCs, but are expensive. Corel programs for PCs are widely used and duplicate most Adobe jobs, though less smoothly. CAD programs are made for building design and are not efficient for free-drawn mosaics. Macromedia packages are also unsuitable.

- Get some help! I despaired of mastering the art of drawing with vectors until I invested in a set of training CDs. Alternatively, you might have a friend who knows the program, or a local college course (not a book). Whichever you use, give yourself lots of time to get the hang of it.

"Exploding Star"
A design produced entirely on the computer. Playing around with the star tool and then colorizing with tones produced a 3-D effect.

5 MORE IDEAS FOR PEBBLE MOSAIC

Since I wrote *The Art of Pebble Mosaics*, I've developed a number of new ideas and techniques in my workshop. Some are exciting and are worth passing on, while others have been quietly forgotten. Some of these "new ideas" have no doubt been done before, but nonetheless I share them with you and hope you find them as interesting as I do.

PEBBLE MOSAICS AND WATER

This is a great combination. Wet pebbles are twice as bright as dry ones, reminiscent of the brilliant colors found in shallow seashore rock pools. William Havey used the idea for the "Pebble Garden" at Dumbarton Oaks in Washington D.C. (see page 112, U.S., Section 2). Shallow water is all that's needed: there's no sense in covering the mosaic with so much water that the shape of the pebbles and even the design gets blurred. In my experience a depth of 2 in (5 cm) is quite sufficient, and has the added advantage that children can play with the water and touch the pebbles in safety. It also avoids the possible horror of small animals drowning.

In a cascade or fountain, the water can be made to ripple over an inclined plane. The light vibrates with the movement of the water, and little splashes and ripples animate the design. Again, too much water only serves to hide the motif, and in this context (moving, rather than still water) I've found that a cover of no more than 1 in (2.5 cm) is best. Multiply this depth by the area of the mosaic, and add the volume of water required for the reservoir and circulatory pipes, to calculate the total for the system.

Plumelike fountainheads provide enough water to stream over a 16 ft (5 m) diameter town mosaic. The water empties into a continuous covered drain at the perimeter. Any rubbish accumulates here and is collected daily as part of the park maintenance schedule. It's a neat solution to the problem created by urban debris in this type of public context. It's also a good resource for city workers who fancy a paddle on hot days! Bradford, Yorkshire, U.K.

FOUNTAINS, POOLS AND CASCADES

To see the mosaic at its best, the water must be kept crystal clear by continuous filtering and cleaning. It's surprising how quickly green algae appears and specks of dust become layers of sludge. Some sophisticated water technology is called for and, fortunately, there are many specialists operating in this field. A typical system will include a pump, storage tank to supply the water, filtration device, dosing or sterilization unit, pipework and the various fountainheads that deliver water over the mosaic. Everything must be watertight and overspill drainage provided.

Unfortunately, all water installations carry a high cost. The pebble mosaic itself will represent only a fraction of the budget, most of which goes on the equipment and the infrastructure required to construct a safe and efficient water-feature. However, the fascination of water and pebbles is universally acknowledged. People love them; and where there's a demand, there's often a will to find the funding.

This shallow pool has a water covering of only 2 in (5 cm)—a safe depth for children and small animals. In fact, the fountain was designed in such a way that small children could lean over the stone surround, dabble in the water and enjoy the simple child-friendly motifs without any danger. The memorial fountain at Dunblane cemetery, Scotland.

Sparkle and movement created by shallow water rippling over the pebble mosaic. The steps in this cascade are inclined at an angle of 18°. Cascade at East Cleveland Hospital, U.K.

A central "bunch" of foaming white water spreads over a mosaic of cavorting fish, and drains into a slot at the perimeter. Fountain at Aldershot memorial garden, Hampshire, U.K.

EXOTIC MATERIALS

I have always been cautious of introducing artificial materials into basic compositions of pebble and stone. After all, putting together different colors and shapes of natural stone is where the craft started. It's only too easy to lose the subtle, subdued appeal of pebblework by introducing fancy "foreigners." But where the subject itself calls for a special effect, small quantities of other materials can often be very effective.

⬆ Colored glass as used in modern Chinese gardens. The glass is broken into rough chunks and appears to be a hard and durable material; presumably a by-product of the Chinese glass industry.

⬆ Detail of another section of pavement in the Guqi Garden. Broken shards of white pottery, roof tiles, circular drainpipes, pieces of glass, and a few pebbles are used to make a free-drawn spiral.

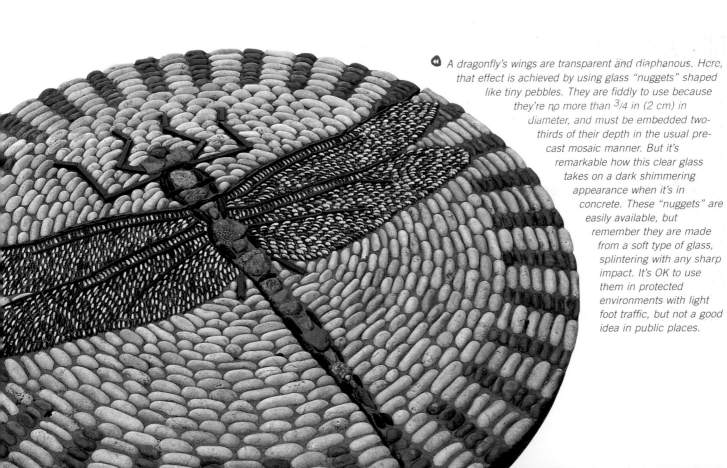

⬅⬅ A dragonfly's wings are transparent and diaphanous. Here, that effect is achieved by using glass "nuggets" shaped like tiny pebbles. They are fiddly to use because they're no more than 3/4 in (2 cm) in diameter, and must be embedded two-thirds of their depth in the usual pre-cast mosaic manner. But it's remarkable how this clear glass takes on a dark shimmering appearance when it's in concrete. These "nuggets" are easily available, but remember they are made from a soft type of glass, splintering with any sharp impact. It's OK to use them in protected environments with light foot traffic, but not a good idea in public places.

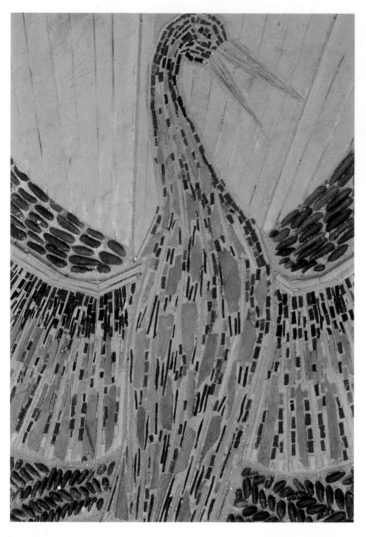

⬆ This phoenix was made to symbolize the revitalization of a site that had once housed metal foundries and engineering works. Strips of stainless steel are interspersed with slate and, for color, glass smalti. Other metals might expand in heat, and crack the mosaic but stainless steel has an almost zero coefficient of expansion.

◆ Chinese pebble mosaic often makes use of ceramic tiles and broken shards of roof tiles and pots. This striking tortoiseshell design is made with hard black and white tiles set on their edge. It goes without saying that all ceramic material used in mosaic paving should be of high-fired stoneware to give long-term durability. Guqi Garden, Shanghai, China.

Two kinds of exotic stone: the turquoise color is amazonite from Russia, and the blue is dumortierite from Brazil. These raw materials can be bought as roughly broken and graded chunks from specialist importers, who supply a huge variety of rocks from around the world. Take care to use only hard, durable types. You'll need a good tumbling machine and tungsten carbide powder to be able to turn them into "pebbles." Both amazonite and dumortierite are too hard to make into really rounded shapes but several days of tumbling will produce smooth angular pieces. These are expensive stones, and are used in such large quantities here because of the nature of the image depicted: St. Neot. The only known image of this obscure 9th-century saint is found on the famous Alfred Jewel, a medieval brooch in which gold filigree separates areas of brilliant blue, green and red enamel. The decision to adapt this lovely design for mosaic led to a search for these particular colors of stone. St.Neots, Cambridgeshire, U.K.

A panel of slate with a resin-filled sandblasted linear "drawing." This idea was developed in order to incorporate informative historical "scenes" into a small mosaic. Pebbles would have no chance of picking out such detail on this scale. The grooves in the slate were blasted as deeply as possible and drilled with tiny holes at 45° to make a "key" for the white resin.

GRINDING AND POLISHING

A wonderful effect can be produced by grinding flat the whole surface of the pebble mosaic. It must first be roughly milled down to produce a completely flat surface, removing about $1/2$ in (1.2 cm) of pebble. Then an industrial polishing machine (known as a "Jenny Lind" in the U.K.) is required to work through a series of diamond grinders until a fine polish is achieved. You'll need the services of a friendly monumental mason for these processes.

Obviously the mosaic must be very strongly made to withstand this mechanical pressure, but the normal precast method described in chapter 3

This ground-and-polished mosaic uses exactly the same stones we often use for outdoor mosaics: a red granite, jasper and slate border; black granite pebbles for the figures and a background of mixed granites. Polishing the ground pebbles shows off their fascinating veined and spotted interior, but still retains their essentially "pebbly" look.

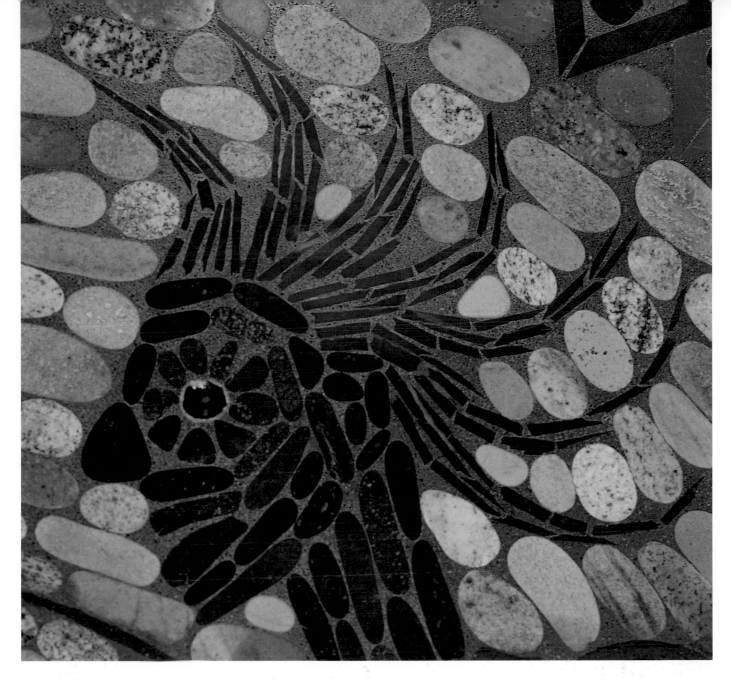

is more than adequate. There is one difference: the mosaic should be made *without* the usual dry sand in the bottom of the mold. Pebbles must be placed so that their crucial point of contact is 1/2 in (1.2 cm) below the final cast surface which, in the absence of sand, will be completely filled with grout. Adding a good quality black concrete tint to the grout will improve the appearance of the background.

The possibilities of this technique are very exciting. Glass and smashed exotic rocks—even flat shaped silhouettes—can be cast directly into the mosaic. The resulting polished panels could be incorporated into patterned granite floors. The field is wide open, but the extra expense of grinding and polishing must be considered. This, coupled with the fact that polished stone is a serious slippery hazard outside and a cold unforgiving surface inside, makes this a product in limited demand.

⬆ *The brilliant shine achieved by polishing the pebbles greatly enhances the stone color. The background stones, all from the same location, would normally appear as uniformly light, creamy colors; but when they're ground and polished, they show an infinite variety of crystalline and veined internal structures.*

6 NEW DEVELOPMENTS IN PEBBLE MOSAIC

NEW COMMERCIAL IDEAS

Sinan Şensoy of Matusan in Turkey has been pioneering new techniques, making pebble mosaic into an almost industrial-scale process: prefabricating pebble mosaic by gluing the pebbles onto a polyester mesh. I say "almost" because the selection and placing of pebbles is still carefully executed by hand.

The mosaic designs are produced ready-assembled, so that the product can be shipped to overseas destinations and assembled by local building contractors. The weight is kept to a minimum, and there is no need for a costly installation by the original makers.

As with any good idea which has commercial potential, these methods have been rapidly taken up and copied, especially in Indonesia and China, but unfortunately the copies are not always of good quality.

⊕ *A pool-side area where pebble tiles have been used. The pebbles are glued flat onto sheets of mesh that are then installed using flexible grout.*

Pebble tiles or "Flat-pebble-on-mesh"

Used in an appropriate situation, the flat-pebble-on-mesh can look very attractive, and is reasonably priced. Suddenly, it's everywhere! But it is not made to last for ever; and, of course, it won't. The pebbles most often used are the beautiful white, pink and green stones which originate in Indonesia. Unfortunately, they are too porous and soft to survive outdoors; and for a steamy bathroom environment would require to be well sealed. Some versions, however, are made using non-porous stones of the typical Chinese varieties (whites, reds and yellows), whilst Matusan also makes use of hard Indian sandstone pebbles. Given careful installation and a protected environment, these products stand a better chance of long-term durability. But the pebblework is only "skin-deep", its thickness is between one third to three quarters of an inch (8–20 mm), and it is held in place, not by its method of construction, but by the strength of the grout alone.

"Vertical" pebble tiles

Another smart idea! Flat pebbles are chopped to a uniform depth and fixed to stand vertically, using PVA, onto the polyester mesh, so that the mesh sheet can be laid down on to a concrete screed and then grouted to create the effect of a traditional mosaic. A good method of cutting the pebbles accurately is required, and Sinan has pioneered a special diamond saw to cut several pebbles at once.

All the intricacy of a traditional in-situ pebble mosaic can be replicated by this method, with the added advantages that the mosaics can be fabricated in the comfort of a workshop, and subsequently shipped world-wide at a relatively low cost.

⊗ *A meander border by Matusan, with cut vertical pebbles glued to mesh, ready for installation with flexible grout.*

⊗ *A large mosaic in the Matusan workshop. The design has been deliberately separated into sections which have an irregular edge in order that the joints, when assembled, will be inconspicuous.*

"Flat" pebble tiles

This is a high-tech version of pebble mosaic in which the pebbles are cut into thin slices and glued onto a polyester net. A cleverly designed miniature gang-saw slices up the pebbles that are arranged in various random patterns and installed in the same manner as pebble tiles. The technique produces a result reminiscent of the "ground and polished" style (see page 78). However, the difficulty of cutting perfect slices limits the range of pebbles which can be used for production. For instance, very hard granite pebbles are impractical, so flat pebble tiles are often limited to more muted tones.

⬆ "Flat" pebble tiles make a smooth stone carpet for an interior floor. This Matusan design has simple flowers on a random background.

⏩ The Gordion Mix by Matusan. Rich colors of very hard sandstone arranged in a carefully composed "random" pattern.

Porcelain "pebbles"

What can be done when the sources of natural pebbles run out? Today, developing countries are happy to gather and export their natural resources, whereas in the more environmentally conscious countries of Europe and the U.S., pebble-gathering is becoming increasingly difficult.

Mehmet Işikli in Antalya, Turkey, has begun to tackle this problem. His answer, however strange, is to "make" pebbles. He has re-thought the whole idea of pebble mosaic, developing the techique of copying natural pebbles in the medium of porcelain. He is convinced that porcelain is stronger than most stones, can be made in any color and, moreover, that the colors are completely permanent and unfading. Another argument is that only 33 lb (15 kg) of porcelain pebble is required per square meter of mosaic in comparison with five times the weight in pebbles, making the cladding of both horizontal and vertical surfaces much easier.

⬆ *Mehmet Işikli placing porcelain "pebbles" in a mosaic design and gluing the pieces on to mesh.*

⬇ *Uniformly sized porcelain "pebbles" create an unrivalled perfection of finish in this mosaic by Mehmet Işikli.*

CERAMICS IN PEBBLE MOSAIC

For many centuries the Chinese made use of ceramics in pebble mosaic, using sections of curved roof-tiles to make their repeat patterns. Many types and colors of tile were placed vertically to outline shapes and fill in areas of the pattern.

Making special ceramic pieces for inclusion in the mosaic takes the idea one step further. The advantages are obvious: high-fired ceramics are very durable, and specially modeled forms extend the possibilities, from small detailed "pebbles" to larger plaques, which can be incorporated into the matrix of pebblework.

The first step is to gain access to a kiln but, more importantly, the knowledge and experience to use it with some degree of precision. Ceramists do indeed spend a lifetime mastering their art. My own exploration into making ceramic pieces for inclusion in pebble mosaics started innocently enough: get a kiln and have a go! Thereafter, I struggled long and hard to achieve the modest results shown here.

A small bird, cast into a wall mosaic, flutters on a branch. It has a matt speckled brown glaze on a stoneware body. The bird was modelled as a bas-relief: 1¼ in (3 cm) deep after firing, with up to ½ in (1 cm) of depth in the modelling. A simple plaster press-mold was made from the original clay model, allowing many pieces to be produced for experimentation with different glazes.

Small images of a fox and horse are encircled by a scroll border in a large mosaic. Ceramics proved very useful in this project as a way of including lots of information without compromising the impact of the overall design (this is a detail of the mosaic at Cholmondeley Castle, featured on page 166).

Pebble mosaics which are made to last for a hundred years and more *must* be durable in all weathers, so ceramic pieces must be frost-proof; and for this, they must be vitrified. This requires that the clay (called the "body") must be either porcelain or stoneware, capable of being fired to a temperature of 1260 °F (680 °C) or higher.

Stoneware bodies, as their name implies, can be rugged and stone-like in appearance, although this can be tempered by the use of colored glazes. I like to aim for effects which look "at home" in combination with pebbles: as though the ceramic intrusion is no more than a special and surprising stone. Through experimentation, I have found several matt and eggshell glazes which blend quite happily with the surface texture of pebbles.

A big advantage of modelling in clay is the fine detail that can be achieved on the pieces which are then introduced into the mosaic. Fine detail can also be carved in stone, but is extremely time-consuming. Here is a simple example: the curved indentations of a small oak leaf can be minutely reproduced as bas-relief in clay; a plaster mold can then be made, and from this, multiple oak-leaves can be pressed. Whereas, to produce a similar leaf in stone is either a long hand-carving process, or expensive blasting or water-jet cutting techniques must be employed.

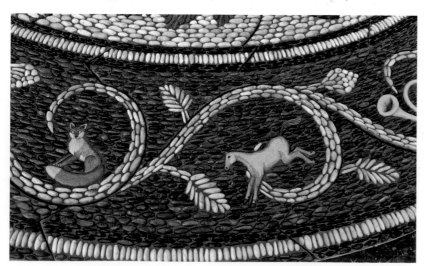

LIGHTING UP THE PAVEMENT

Illuminating a pebble mosaic at night extends the period of time in which the mosaic can be enjoyed and, if well designed, can impart a wonderful atmosphere and glamour to the surroundings. However, incorporating the light source into the actual mosaic presents some difficulties. Technical and electrical wizardry has a shorter life-expectancy than straightforward pebble mosaic.

There are several ways to incorporate light sources into a mosaic pavement: LEDs, fiber-optic cables and specially designed fittings. The choice depends on the site, the expectations of the client, the threat of vandalism and projected wear and tear.

In the design shown below, Janette Ireland based her choice of LEDs on considerations of cost and the likelihood of vandalism. They were connected directly to an adjacent street lighting supply: a relatively cheap and simple solution, and one that guaranteed lighting-up times.

Installation was long and fiddly: cables were laid before the paving, and the bulbs were pushed up through pre-formed holes in the mosaic. These lights, supplied by a specialist firm in various colors, were encased in protective glass sleeves. For additional security Janette obtained extra pieces of toughened glass 8 mm thick, which were held in place by brass tubes which fitted over the LEDs in slots in the mosaic and sealed with silicone. They gave good protection and also acted as lenses, magnifying the lighting effect at night. It's a good idea and looks great, but its future might be limited. Despite a guarantee of 10 years for the LEDs, it's inevitable that a tricky replacement operation must be anticipated.

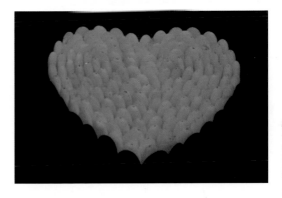

⬆ *Expensive, but what a good idea! Sinan Şensoy has fabricated a custom mold for these "glow-in-the-dark pebbles". They absorb sunlight by day and emit a bright glow by night. Sinan expects them to last for at least one decade. A specialist firm produced the "pebbles" which are formed from a special compound of phosphorescent powder mixed with epoxy resin and quartz powders, and then hardened under pressure and heat.*

⬅ *Eyes that come to life at night! LEDs are fitted into the mosaic through holes cut through the pre-cast mosaic slabs. This detail is from a large mosaic by Janette Ireland in Barrow-in-Furness, U.K., which features 25 sea creatures with glowing eyes, all designed in workshops with local children.*

Around the World

6 PEBBLE MOSAIC TRADITIONS FROM AROUND THE WORLD

This chapter is about the different kinds of pebble mosaic to be found around the world. I am always surprised how the basic concept of pebblework is approached in so many different ways by different pairs of hands. Even two people working on similar projects will make individual choices, producing mosaics that are recognizably different. Similarly, function, culture and materials all contribute greatly to the final effect, resulting in an enormous diversity of approach across the world.

So let's hop continents and centuries to take in this panorama. This won't be a comprehensive survey because I know there's much more to be discovered; but I'm hoping that you'll be amazed, as I am, at the variety and beauty of all the different styles that are shown here. For those who are involved in the actual process of making pebbleworks, there's a wealth of good ideas for you to take in.

▶▶ *Looking closely at the early pebble mosaics right and opposite, you can see that the small pebbles are rounded, but not particularly well shaped, and selected primarily for their size and color. They are widely spaced, obviously pressed into the surface. The spaces between have been well filled to make the floor as flat as possible. The measurements are exact, the lines perfectly straight. The accuracy is impressive. Guides and rulers will have been used; and possibly a squared-up cartoon on papyrus in order to draft the central figured motif.*

Previous pages: (main photo) "The Grotto" by Lorna Jordan, the Waterworks Garden, Renton, Washington; (detail) "Theodora" by Christine Desmond.

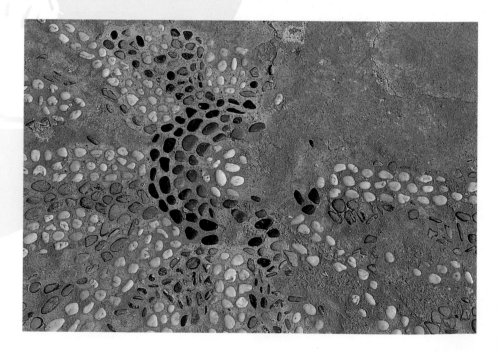

EARLY GREEK PEBBLE MOSAICS

The ancient Greeks had simple tools, no technology, limited materials and no cement, but inventive minds cannot be stopped. Wonderful things can still be made, whatever the means.

Living in expanding and prosperous cities, the early Greeks were a sophisticated people with a highly developed aesthetic sense, who surrounded themselves with beautiful things. It was only natural that they should develop decorative flooring techniques alongside their interests in all the other arts and sciences.

Olynthos

The ancient city of Olynthos in northern Greece was one of the 32 cities of Chalkidiki that formed an alliance against Athens. For a century the city grew in economic and political power until it was finally destroyed by Philip II of Macedonia in 348 B.C.

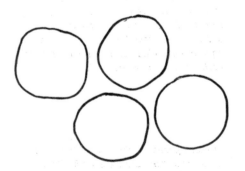

The size of the pebbles used at Olynthos.

▶▶ An impressive excavation at Olynthos. At present, the foundations of 60 houses can be seen: only one-tenth of the original city of five to six thousand inhabitants. Its uncompromising grid pattern was laid out by Hippodamus, famous for his early town planning. Here's one of several surviving pebble mosaics (dated c.400 B.C.) in the "andron," or principal reception room of a typical house. It depicts Bellerophon killing the chimera, a popular theme of masculine daring from Greek mythology. The scroll-pattern border is precisely drawn with an acanthus in each corner and a swastika-type meander around the edges.

▶▶ It's a great design, which I've tried to make clearer in this drawing. It might have been copied from paintings or pottery, and it shows that artists were involved at some point in the design. The choice of a noble subject, balanced drawing of the figures and precision of the decorative framework all indicate a sophistication of approach. Pebble mosaic is no longer a mere functional floor-covering. It has become an art form.

Pella—another leap forward

North of Olynthos was the powerful kingdom of Macedonia. King Archelaos (whose son Philip was later to sack Olynthos) founded his new capital, Pella, around 400 B.C. He created a cultural honey pot, inviting famous artists and intellectuals to the palace: among them the playwright Euripides and the painter Zeuxis. Xenophon described Pella as "greatest of the cities of Macedonia," and its fame spread throughout the known world, following the conquests of Alexander the Great.

Little remains of the city today, but some of the pebble mosaics that once adorned the wealthy houses of the king's court have survived, dated 325–300 B.C. They are made using the same pressed-in technique as Olynthos, and display similar mythological scenes and decorative borders. But the artistry is so much more sophisticated, and the craftsmanship greatly refined, showing that there was much artistic development in the century or less that separates the two styles.

▶ *The size of pebbles used by Gnosis.*

▼ *Gnosis used such tiny pebbles! They are the size of pea gravel, about $^3/_8$ in (1 cm) in diameter. He needed this tiny scale to achieve the delicate modeling of the head. The figures are drawn with careful attention to anatomical detail and musculature in order to present an ideal of virile manhood. In the quest for realism there is a foreshortening of the arms, and the creation of 3-D depth by tonal grading of the pebbles. The shading uses only two main tones, with a darker area for the deep shadows behind the body. It's a very limited palette for such ambitions, and accounts for a certain stiffness of expression. Still, it's meticulous work, painstakingly rendered. The artist signed the mosaic like a painting "ΓΝΩΣΙΣ ΕΠΟΗΣΕΝ" (Gnosis made it). We have to assume that he was an accomplished painter who applied his skill to the design and technical improvements of this mosaic at Pella. (See also the illustration on page 216 of the Gazetteer.)*

⬆ *A wonderful border of scrolls, tendrils and flowers, surrounding "The Deer Hunt" at Pella, Greece. It is perhaps the most decorative floral pattern to be made in pebble mosaic. The stylization of the plant forms fits comfortably with the shading used to create depth in the spirals.*

⬇ *Dionysus, a Greek god, is a recurring motif on fourth-century B.C. vase painting. Despite the large scale of this mosaic, 9 ft (2.75 m) square, the design may well be copied from a much smaller original. The leopard (also described as a cheetah or spotted panther) has a particularly strange look, the result perhaps of many generations of copying: growing more and more stylized at each remove. Of particular interest is the use of lead strips around the face, and the fired terracotta curls in the hair, which add definition.*

Roman mosaics

The use of pebbles as the predominant material for mosaic was gradually superseded by the well-known Roman style that soon spread throughout the Empire. The technique involved the use of tesserae, small cubes of cut stone or ceramic, which greatly increased the range of available colors. The mosaics began to rival painting in their elaborateness of detail. Today, they are a source of inspiration for their bold patterns, and an object lesson in floor design.

The expensive tesserae mosaics were taking over in the rich Roman houses, but pebble mosaics, in their own humble way, were still serviceable enough for local purposes. This long-standing tradition in Mediterranean countries, with its regional variations, probably derives from the influence of successive waves of Arab expansion in the area.

ANDALUCIA

The Umayyad caliphate was established in Spain in A.D. 711 with Granada as its capital. There, after five centuries of continuous Arab rule, the great palace and gardens of the Alhambra were constructed and the particular garden art of Moorish culture developed. It was characterized by its formal layouts of clipped hedges, shady colonnades, scented plants and cooling waters in gently flowing rills, reflective pools and basins. Many of the paths were pebble mosaic in black and white. Since all human representation in art was frowned upon in Islamic law, imagery had to be either floral or geometric (with occasional exceptions, probably of recent date). It's an ideal formula: the pebblework complementing the stylish formality of the architecture and planting.

⊙ A view of the Generalife gardens at the Alhambra Palace, Granada, Spain. Simple large-scale patterns in black and white pebbles add decorative effect to the paths and intersections, contrasting with the sculptural topiary and fountain.

⊙ Large-scale scrollwork makes a lively path in the Generalife garden. The long black pebbles are laid in herringbone pattern and infilled with random rounded white pebbles. This formula established a style of pebble mosaic that has persisted to the present day in the plazas, courtyards and pavements of Andalucia: in Cordoba, Seville, Ronda, Malaga and very many smaller towns and villages.

TURKEY

At the other end of the Mediterranean Sea, during the 13th century, the vast Muslim Ottoman Empire was established with the city of Constantinople as its chosen capital. It flourished for six centuries, during which a particular style of Ottoman and Seljuk scrollwork and motifs developed. They are found in all the decorative arts of this area, including pebble mosaics.

Pebble mosaic with star-forms and diamond patterns decorates a shady colonnade in a courtyard of the Topkapi Palace, Istanbul (formerly Constantinople), Turkey. This pebblework has probably been restored many times, a heritage from the heyday of Mehmet the Conqueror's rule from 1451–81.

GREECE AND THE ISLANDS

There is a long-established tradition of pebblework on the Greek islands, in both courtyards and interiors. From the 13th century, the island of Rhodes was an important center for the crusading knights of St. John, and early pebble mosaics have been dated from this time. A later conquest by the sultan Suleyman the Magnificent, in the great siege of 1522–23, brought in an Ottoman influence. Pebblework has continued to the present day and good examples can be found on many of the islands, including Rhodes, Santorini, Spetses, Chios, Lesbos and Symi.

A palm tree makes a good motif on a small scale.

A modern rendition of pebblework in Rhodes town. The boom in tourism (Rhodes absorbs a tenfold increase in its population during the holiday season) has revitalized the use of decorative pebble mosaics. The forecourt to this bank shows the cross of the Order of St. John alternating with some attractive island motifs.

Greek pebblework enlivens the interiors of traditional buildings as well as courtyards and public spaces. This wonderful floor in tiny black and white pebbles is in the church at Archangelos on Rhodes. The zigzag pattern seems surprisingly modern for this building, while the floral patterns show an Ottoman influence. You might think that a textured surface would be inconvenient for a public building; but here the floor is beautifully maintained by a band of local ladies with brushes and pans (some have left their tools in the picture).

PORTUGAL

It's not exactly pebblework, but the stone mosaics of Portugal have such distinction of design and skill that I include them here. They are not only a fusion of Moorish geometry and Celtic interlacing, but also display bold optical patterns that are entirely their own—a unique style that nonetheless transplanted successfully to the many Portuguese colonies around the world.

The mosaic pavements are made with small cubes of calcareous limestone and black basalt, both abundantly available and very suitable for hard-wearing pavements. The stones are shaped by hand with chisel hammers and tapped, one by one, into a dry mix of gritty sand and cement. This is skilled work, requiring months of training. Unfortunately it's not well paid, so great efforts have to be made to preserve the craft.

▶ A favorite Portuguese motif: a striking wave pattern representing the sea and celebrating Portugal's glorious era of exploration in the 15th century, when Prince Henry "the Navigator" sent expeditions on long exploratory voyages. The Rossio, Lisbon.

▶ Crisp black and white paving patterns in Porto, Portugal. The patterns are achieved by means of wooden stencils, carpenter-made and kept for ongoing repairs. The stencils are laid on the ground and the white background precisely fitted to the gaps between. When the stencil is lifted, the black areas are filled with the same attention to detail.

⬆ *Today, modern mosaics are being created by the Portuguese artist Éduardo Néry, continuing the tradition of inventive design coupled with an old-established craft. This bold new work in the Praça do Município in Lisbon is by Néry. It measures 198 ft x 257 ft (60 m x 78 m). Commissioned by the Camera Municípal de Lisbõa, it was completed in 1999.*

MADEIRA

Madeira was discovered by Portugal in 1419, and subsequently developed as a colony. Despite a checkered history of occupation by the Spanish and British, Madeira has retained its Portuguese character, architectural style and pavement mosaics. Locally quarried material is not plentiful in Madeira, so it's not surprising that pebbles predominate over cut stones. The same precision is applied to both techniques, using templates to make accurate and stylish patterns.

◀ ⬙Opposite and above: Intertwined floral scrolls echo the Manueline curves in the stonework at the entrance of this church in Caniço, Madeira. The fine pebblework enlivens an otherwise stark exterior. Very tiny pebbles are used, less than 1 in (2.5 cm), giving a good definition to the pattern.

◀ A wonderful path leading up to the Residencia Santa Clara in Funchal, Madeira. The elaborate interlacing pattern recalls the influence of Celtic knotwork, which is deeply ingrained in Portuguese culture.

A lovely flight of steps in the garden at Isola Bella on Lake Maggiore. Scroll patterns in black, white and red pebbles decorate each step and make a lively contrast with the heavy granite balustrade and bright red and green plants.

The sunken garden at the Villa Gamberaia, Settignano, Florence, Italy. The walls are encrusted with stone textures and niches housing terracotta statues. Pebble mosaicwork adorns the pathways around the upper terrace.

ITALY

The Renaissance in Italy encouraged a renewed interest in the arts of ancient Greece and Rome. All classical art forms were sought after, studied and copied; and new palaces and gardens were constructed on a grand scale to display the collections. The Nymphaeum (a decorative fountain, sacred to

nymphs) of classical times was reinvented and became the grotto of Renaissance gardens, often decorated with rustic limestone, shells and pebbles, and animated with waterworks. At the center of many great European trade routes, Renaissance Italy was a cultural melting pot. A fusion of garden styles took place, characterized by elaborate architectural works: pools and tanks, balustrading, formal parterres, staircases, statuary and grottoes. Many fine pebble mosaics appeared in gardens during this period, with classical motifs and scrollwork, as well as geometric patterns.

❷ A striking geometric pattern using three different tones of pebbles. Villa Medicea di Castello, Florence, Italy.

One of the best of these gardens is at the Villa Gamberaia on the outskirts of Florence. Made about 1710, it is well furnished with pebbleworks, both on its paths and on the walls of its nymphacum. Twenty years ago I found, in a book of Italian gardens, a photograph of one of these mosaics which showed a stork, beautifully made in tiny black and white pebbles. This photograph was one of the major inspirations that led to my working in pebbles. Years later, I was able to visit the garden myself but, sadly, the little stork was covered in moss and hardly visible. Despite the lavish care bestowed on the topiary and lawns, and the restoration of the architectural stonework of the Nymphaeum, the owners are showing little regard for the care of the pebble paths. It's a salutary tale: art on the floor is often ignored.

The finest achievement in Renaissance pebble mosaics is to be found in the Nymphaeum at the Villa Borromeo Visconti Litta at Lainate, near Milan. Count Pirro I (1560–1605), who built the Nymphaeum, was a true patron of the arts, gathering together the best craftspeople and artists, and enthusiastically calling for experimentation in a wide variety of styles. Water-jokes abound: ingenious concealed sprays, triggered by hidden operators, surprise the visitor with a light

In one of the rooms, called the Egg Room, pebble mosaic is applied to 3-D scallop shells set into the architectural framework of fossil limestone.

Paths around the Nymphaeum are decorated with pebble mosaic, from which hidden fountains, triggered by an enthusiastic band of volunteers, surprise the unwary visitor. One of the operators is lurking in the picture; the controls are concealed in the niches.

wetting; fountains drive kinetic sculptures; waterfalls pour from the ceiling. The novel hydraulic system was a wonder of its day, and has recently been restored to its former glory.

The pebble mosaics have been restored after many years of neglect, and they too show a bold experimental approach. They cover not only entire floors, but walls and ceilings too, in the 11 "gallery" rooms where an art collection was displayed. There are elaborate repeating patterns, from acanthus scrolls to strong geometric designs, all made in tiny black limestone and white quartz. Restoration has revealed how the designs were originally painted directly onto the walls in black lines with washes of gray and white to indicate the fill color. A top layer of mortar was applied, section by section, so that the design could be copied and the pebbles pressed into each area.

In the ceiling mosaics, more interesting experimentation took place. The artist Camillo Procaccini worked in six of the rooms from 1587–89. His usual occupation was as a painter of sacred subjects; but here, and in the frescoes he painted in the villa itself, he was encouraged to let his imagination range freely over more profane material. There are satyrs, dragons, unicorns and what were known as "grotesques": figures that metamorphize from one state to another. Leaves turn into nymphs, a dragon emerges from a shell. This was unusual for a sacred artist, but more extraordinary still, Procaccini is credited with pioneering an innovative

⬆ *The technique used in making the mosaics is seen clearly in this area of wall, which has been preserved to show the process. The original underpainting, like a fresco, can be seen. A thin layer of mortar was then applied into which the pebbles were pressed. Note the small size of the pebbles: less than $^1/_2$ in (1.5 cm)*

◀ *Walls, ceiling and floor opposite are all decorated with pebble mosaics in the magnificent gallery rooms of the Nymphaeum of the Villa Litta. Here acanthus-leaf scrolls in tiny black and white pebbles adorn the walls; while on the ceiling, pictures in pebbles, by Procaccini, show griffins, dragons, unicorns and "grotesques" arranged in a decorative framework. The "pictures" were originally colored with pigments, but these have long since faded.*

103

pebble mosaic technique. He would make an entire mosaic in white pebbles, the figures being visible only by the flow of the lines, and then proceed to literally paint the mosaic with colors. The result may have been brilliant at the time but, unhappily, all that can be seen now are traces of faded color and the indistinct forms of creatures in an exuberant but unclear design. What happened, I guess, is that Procaccini, the proud muralist, became frustrated with the black and white discipline of the Nymphaeum and decided to try for color and fluidity, at whatever cost.

The overall design of this Nymphaeum has come a long way from the original ancient Roman concept of a single grotto. It has developed into a large and splendid building for cool recreation in the summer heat. It was designed, in addition, to house a valuable art collection of statues and paintings. The 11 pebble mosaic rooms are arranged either side of a grand octagonal hall, the Atrium of the Four Winds. Its pillars and arches are formed of craggy fossil limestone, in contrast to the sophistication of the antique statuary and mosaic panels.

The east wing of the Nymphaeum houses the Ancient Grotto, a semicircular tunnel made to appear like a natural cave with limestone rock formations, artfully designed with niches and pebblework panels contrasting with shell and tufa. Lit through holes in the cavern roof, statues of water nymphs are posed in shallow pools while gentle showers animate the scene.

A quite different style of pebble

mosaic can be seen in the Great Grotto, a new gallery that was added in 1795. The mosaics are like paintings of the Romantic period: idealized landscape scenes are set within rustic rock frames; swallows even fly in the "sky" overhead.

Both the Villa and Nymphaeum at Lainate were much admired and visited throughout the 17th and 18th centuries. The concept of a series of rooms, decorated with pebble mosaics and designed to house an art collection, became fashionable for those with the means to build and stock them. One hundred years later, in the Renaissance palace at Isola Bella on Lake Maggiore, Count Borromeo copied the idea, but with far less discretion and originality. It is no overstatement to describe the Villa Litta Nymphaeum as a uniquely inventive original creation.

◀◀ The Atrium of the Four Winds opposite is a lofty octagonal hall at the center of the Nymphaeum at Villa Litta. A statue of Venus is one of several classical sculptures that inhabit its arches. Pebble mosaic border panels are integrated into the rustic travertine architecture, and the pebble floor is regularly sprinkled with water from the hidden fountains.

◀◀ One of the wall mosaics in the Atrium of the Four Winds. Made with broken fragments of different colors of marble, this female grotesque has such a modern look that it's hard to believe she was made in the 16th century. The fashion for grotesques was common during the Renaissance, and is explored extensively throughout the villa. In this instance, a woman is transforming into the branches of a tree, with a broken branch for an arm, and a crown of leaves.

The Villa Litta lies about 11 miles (18 km) from the center of Milan and is open on weekends, April–October. For current visiting hours see www.amicivillalitta.it.

⬆ *The Ancient Grotto is a labyrinth of cavelike tunnels housing more statues, regularly sprayed with showering fountains. Small but elaborate pebble mosaic panels of grotesque animals and scrollwork are set into the walls and ceiling.*

◀ *A different style of pebble mosaic is seen in the Great Grotto in the Villa Litta. Made in 1795, at the height of the Romantic era, the pebble technique has been adapted to realize a series of idealized landscape scenes, set into the rustic architecture like views from a window.*

UNITED KINGDOM

The cobbling of Old England still holds a place in many villages in rural areas. While it is often plain and functional, there are occasional examples of decorative patterning, simple motifs and dates. Villages situated close to

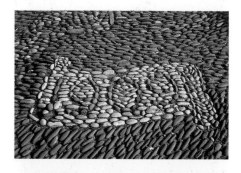

⬆ *Examples of traditional pebblework at the fishing village of Lytham. Top is a nice pavement detail—nearly a century old and still looking good—and the 150-year-old pavement above reveals the secret of a pebble mosaic's durability: well-selected pebbles, close-packed, vertically placed and protected on all sides.*

⯈ *The entrance to Bickleigh Castle, Devon, U.K., was constructed by Italian prisoners of war; homesick, perhaps, and remembering the gardens of Tuscany. The pattern of shell shapes is original, however, made with local river stones, forming an interesting setting for this fine old building.*

 Some blue flints have been "knapped" or split in half to make a contrasting flat surface to the pebblework.

 A delightful garden area of an old house in Sandwich, Kent, U.K. Rounded flints in blue and white are combined with old red bricks to make a pretty centerpiece. This is another picture that inspired me to "have a go" at pebble mosaic myself. The way in which the slim bricks-on-edge circulate from the center adds a spin and frisson to this otherwise static design.

beaches will often have pebblework to be discovered in hidden corners, and country houses will sometimes have stable-yards where the "cobbling" has been carefully designed and made.

Two of the pebble mosaics from the U.K. shown here are directly influenced by the Mediterranean styles: the idea of decorative pebblework has been applied to a British scene and made in local materials.

This is the story behind the mosaic above: an old lady who lived in the house during the 1950s employed a Cypriot chauffeur. As this lady became older and more infirm, the chauffeur found his days increasingly idle. To pass the time, he drew on his Cypriot memories and planned and made a pebble mosaic. He collected matching rounded flints from a nearby beach and cleverly adjusted his pattern to accommodate the red brick paving common to this area.

UNITED STATES

The New World took some time to establish its own style of landscape design and garden art. In the rush to develop the country and exploit its enormous natural resources, there was little time for the arts, and styles were imported wholesale from Europe. Inevitably elements from England, France, Spain and Italy predominated.

So it's not surprising to find pebble mosaics in some of the gardens built by the rich entrepreneurs of the 20th century.

One such example is the garden of the Vanderbilt Museum, in Centreport, N.Y., a mansion built in the Spanish Revival style for William K. Vanderbilt between 1910 and 1936, then known as "Eagle's Nest." The mosaics were developed by Louis Hanousek who, in 1936, was employed at the mansion by the architect Ronald Pearce. Hanousek invented the designs and oversaw the work with enthusiasm, helping to figure out the pebble details. Stones came from nearby Asharoken Beach. The technique is similar to that of southern Spain, using herringbone patterns in black pebbles.

At Dumbarton Oaks, in Washington D.C., the well-known landscape designer Beatrix Farrand created a garden for Mildred and Robert Woods Bliss over the 20-year period between 1921 and 1941. She achieved a fusion of Spanish, Italian and English styles within a North American

◐ ◑ ◑ Pebble mosaic borders, with a variety of designs, are placed on each side of the broad approach-road, complementing the sumptuous Spanish-style architecture of the Vanderbilt Museum.

110

setting. Sculptural balustrading, terraces, walks and formal flowerbeds are set in a richly wooded landscape. Her approach to pebblework within the garden was quite particular, choosing small areas in which to integrate the mosaic with sculpture and seating. In the 1960s, some time after Farrand's death, Mildred Woods Bliss commissioned William Havey to design a large pebble garden to replace the old tennis court.

❯❯ *The elegant water parterre known as the "Pebble Garden" at Dumbarton Oaks. Shallow water covers the swirling lines of Mexican pebbles, which are contrasted with arabesques of pale stone and raised beds of green plants. An immense wheatsheaf and carved cornucopia lie at one end, and a fountain with statuary at the other; while the base of the pool is made with pebblework in great sweeping curves. The design is reminiscent of Italian and Portuguese gardens, but there is some new thinking in the way the water levels are arranged. The idea of overlaying the pebblework with shallow water, in contrast to the raised parterre, is something previously unseen.*

Near Santa Barbara in California, there is a remarkable garden, Lotusland, that is the creation of Madame Ganna Walska, a wealthy opera singer and socialite. She was a determined woman, whose original design ideas and passion for rare plants permeate the garden. The pebble mosaic at Lotusland owes nothing to Europe except perhaps a knowledge of the craft. It is pure North American: a new genre of abstract decorative design.

More recently, contemporary artists in the U.S. have become interested in the medium (see the features in chapter 8 on Lorna Jordan and Christine Desmond).

These unusual abstract designs, in pebble mosaic, border the paths to the fern garden at Lotusland, Santa Barbara. They were designed by Jim Minah and made by Oswald da Ros in 1969. He had a problem finding pebbles in all the required colors, and solved it by tumbling chunks of colored stone in a cement mixer.

CHINA

For over a millennium, the civilization of China developed independently, and unknown to the West. Apart from trade via the Silk Road, there was little contact until the 17th century. Later, in the 18th century, the fashion for "chinoiserie" developed; but only in recent years has the country opened up to allow us to see for ourselves the artistic treasures, monuments and gardens of this amazing culture. Everything is on a vast scale: the territory, the cities, the population, the history and the extent of China's social and artistic achievements. It is startling to learn how advanced Chinese civilization was at a time when parts of the West were, by comparison, extremely backward, even primitive.

⬆ *Pebble mosaic patterns carpet the winding path between rocks in the Xu Yuan garden in Nanjing, China. Piled limestone boulders make fantastic rock walls suggesting mountain scenery. The pebblework shows one of the many repeating patterns tailored like a smooth carpet between the rocks.*

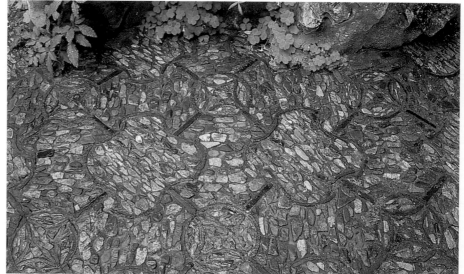

▶▶ *Another repeating pattern made with a latticework of curved and straight tile segments. Many different kinds of pebbles and rock fragments are used for infill: here, a ginger-colored sandstone with white limestone. The mosaic is tailored exactly to the surrounding rock wall, and green plants are encouraged to inhabit the crevices.*

▶▶ *A little surprise under your feet on an otherwise plain rock mosaic path in Liu Yuan, Suzhou, China. Roof tiles, contrasting pebbles, white ceramic shards and a few pieces of bright blue glass are the materials used.*

△ *View from a garden pavilion in Shizilin (the Lion Grove Garden), Suzhou, China. Just one glimpse of the many enchanting views and vistas, which are so contrived that they change at every turn. The "cracked ice" pattern on the delicate wooden screen mingles with the tracery of the trees. The same pattern is found in pebblework (see page 197).*

◄◄ *A patterned path leads to the lovely Moon Gate in Liu Yuan (the Garden of Lingering) at Suzhou, China. This pattern is formed with segments of curved tile, making a decorative latticework. It's an attractive technique: not only is the pattern given sharp definition, but the lattice of curved tile is also a useful setting-out device for the mosaic construction. The tile segments are put in place first and leveled, and then the panels are filled in with pebbles of different colors.*

One of the many Chinese characters meaning "longevity." Bats fly around it. Pebble, tiles-on-edge, ceramic shards and here, unusually, ceramic disks like small pot lids have been pressed into service.

A close-up of a bat and seedpods. Bats are a popular image in Chinese art because their name sounds like the word for luck. The mosaicists have improvised with the random seedpods at the margins, turning the tiles into leaf shapes.

The early Shang Dynasty, from the 16th century B.C., was the first to dominate the country. They cast in bronze, wrote in characters and developed the technology of irrigation and flood control. China was at the forefront of civilization. They invented paper and used it widely for a thousand years before the West learned the secret. But they were not entirely insular. Hostile northern tribes were a constant threat and encouraged the development of large fortified enclosures with high walls. This functional architecture gradually gave rise to a taste for natural landscapes that were contained and ordered within the confines of a dwelling; and to the creation of gardens for refreshment and contemplation.

Gardenmakers sought to evoke China's monumental landscape in miniature. Winding paths created complex journeys among jagged rocks, ingeniously contriving unexpected views and new vistas. Strategically placed pavilions or tiny kiosks, with connecting verandas and footbridges over lakes and canals, offered retreats for study, art and domestic ceremonials. Within the artificial wilderness, gardeners strove to create a balance of "yin" and "yang" to achieve spiritual harmony.

Spiritual life in China was dominated by the parallel religions of Confucianism and Daoism. The one stressed the importance of personal subordination to authority and the ethic of hard work, while the other sought an escape from society, and a mystical union with nature. Together they mapped an ideal lifestyle, beginning with an active urban

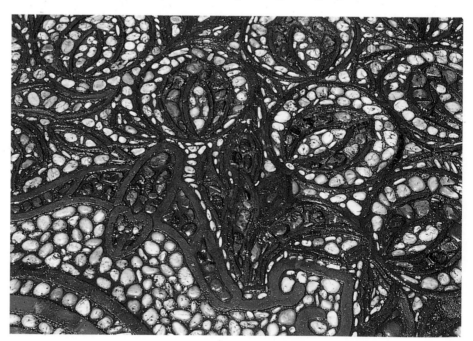

This celebrated garden, the He Yuan at Yangzhou, shows how the Chinese love to bring water into the garden, its moist and feminine yin element contrasting with the masculine yang of the rockwork and buildings. The unattractively stagnant water seems to present no problem. The pebble mosaic is unusual, suggesting buds or seedpods connecting to branchlike tracery. Made with black roof tiles, black pebbles and bright white quartz, it is entirely random except for the straight lines bordering the building.

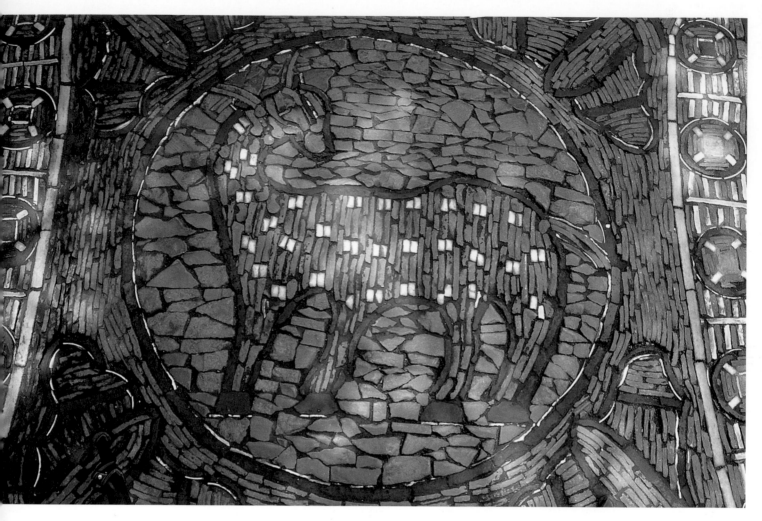

career in public service and ending with a contemplative retirement to the country.

The communion with nature is further reinforced by the great importance attached to natural stone. Stones were worshipped in ancient China for their supernatural properties and, even today, hold a very special place in the Chinese psyche. They have always been collected and command high prices, particularly the type of craggy contorted limestone often seen in gardens. They are placed with infinite care to achieve a correct balance with the opposite elements of calm water, smooth surfaces and green foliage. Sometimes entire rock mountains are built with internal passageways and caverns, dwarfing the buildings. Rocks form the infrastructure of the garden; but our concern is with their opposite, the yang to their yin, the smooth feminine pebble as distinct from the masculine rock.

Chinese pebbleworks function as a continuous groundscape, tailored like a patterned carpet between the rock walls, mountains and monoliths. In the West, mosaic floors tend to associate with architecture, centering on a space, with a middle and edges and borders. In China the mosaic surface rolls out seamlessly, changing pattern with a change in the surrounding

An allover pattern of offset triangles, edged in stone and filled with brown pebbles and blue glass. It makes a softly patterned carpet in this courtyard in Zhou Zheng Yuan (the Garden of the Unsuccessful Politician) in Suzhou, China. One of the famous gardens of Suzhou, it is often visited by large parties of Chinese travelers enjoying their heritage, along with a few foreign tourists.

landscape, placing the occasional significant motif in a quiet corner or at an intersection or, apparently, quite randomly.

Knowing just how much labor is involved in making such large areas of mosaic, I'm impressed by the consistency of skill and teamwork to achieve these results. The large selection of different allover patterns that can be found in the bible of Chinese garden design, the *Yuan Yeh*, first published in 1634, are still in use today.

STONE PICTURE MOSAICS IN THE "BACK YARD"

There is a very special form of pebble mosaic in part of the Imperial Palace (the Forbidden City) in Beijing. As far as I know, it is unique. A series of garden areas known as the "Back Yard" are tucked away on the north side. A place of relaxation from the stresses of office, this was where the English tutor to the last emperor had his cottage. The garden paths are arranged on a rectilinear grid pattern between symmetrically placed buildings with trees, pools, a waterfall and a rock mountain. All these paths are bordered with small elaborate mosaic panels. In all we counted more than 800, each

The mosaics are slowly revealed using water and elbow grease. There are so many, mainly Chinese, people now visiting the Forbidden City that the mosaics are dirty and largely unseen. My interest in them attracted plenty of attention.

Such incredible detail in small stone bas-relief! It's interesting to see how all the "drawing" of the picture is achieved by the use of carved stone elements. The pebbles themselves are uniform, small sized, randomly placed and fit the area like a lacquerwork infill.

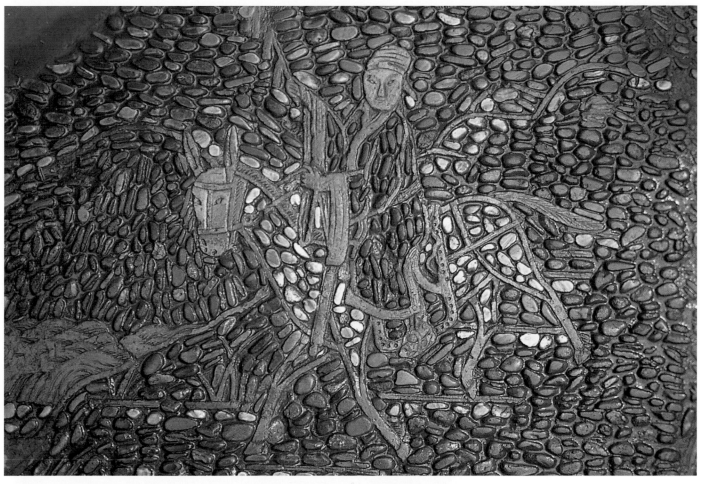

A picture mosaic from the "Back Yard" of the Imperial Palace, Beijing, China. Although this figure with horse measures only 12 in (30 cm), delicate strips of stone have been sawn to delineate the perimeter, while the heads have been carved in subtle bas-relief.

This close-up shows the delicacy of carving on the man's face and hand, and the brightly colored tiny pebbles.

measuring 18 in x 48 in (45 cm x 120 cm), encompassing an astonishing array of subjects: trees, flowers, animals, interiors and people engaged in all sorts of activities, from domestic occupations to warfare, from relaxation to ceremonial parades.

The panels are remarkable for the delicacy of their carved stone bas-relief. Sometimes it makes a fretwork outlining areas of pebbles, while in other panels fine bas-relief silhouettes are set within a background of tiny

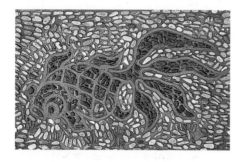

⬆ A familiar type of fish in China, the popular fancy carp. Just one of hundreds of subjects on show in the "Back Yard."

⬇ A plum tree depicted in Chinese style. With its typical cloud, it might have been copied from a carved wooden lacquered screen. The artist has carved fragile silhouettes with bas-relief and laid them into a background of plum-colored pebbles.

pebbles. Despite the layers of grime and dust, the jewel-like colors of many of the pebbles can still be seen; they may indeed be semiprecious stones such as jasper and malachite. Now that all access restrictions have been lifted to the Forbidden City, the people of China are flocking to the Imperial Palace and taking great pride in their heritage. Unfortunately, they come in such numbers that the floorscape can hardly be seen, let alone kept clean. Let's hope that, as restoration proceeds, some of these remarkable mosaic pictures will be cleaned and preserved from too much wear.

Was this one of those legendary extravagances of an emperor: to demand that stone "paintings" should be made by his craftspeople and laid out underfoot? They are reminiscent of metalware relief panels, carved screens, paintings on silk and lacquerware. Nevertheless, the artistry is enchanting and the skill displayed quite marvelous, setting a benchmark for our aspirations.

Another style of mosaic from the "Back Yard" of the Imperial Palace. The bold design of flowers and leaves employs carefully sawn strips of stone to separate the brightly colored red, plum and green pebbles from the white background.

A well-bearded Chinese gentleman stretches a hammock in the garden. Plum, green, black and white pebbles are used.

A picture mosaic that might have been the subject of a tray or screen in another medium. A set-piece interior arrangement, including a storage unit, mirror, fan and rock sculpture, topped by a bowl of fruit.

8 CONTEMPORARY PEBBLE MOSAICISTS

A great range of styles and methods make up the contemporary world scene in pebble mosaics. Again, the survey is not exhaustive and I apologize to those artists around the globe whom I've not yet met, and who are therefore not included. To those artists who are represented here I owe thanks for their many generous contributions of photographs and information that makes this rich mixture possible.

We begin with two famous artists, not best known for their pebblework, who nonetheless made something fine and original in the medium. They are both now dead, but their work is so modern and relevant that they are included here alongside contemporary pebble mosaicists.

New mosaic work by Matusan. The traditional Ottoman patterns are given a contemporary look by the use of a half-tone background motif.

CANARY ISLANDS

CÉSAR MANRIQUE (1919–92)

"To create with absolute freedom, without fear or recipes, comforts the soul and opens a road to the joy of living."

Manrique established his international reputation as a modern abstract painter in the artistic hot spots of Madrid, Paris and New York. Returning home to his beloved island of Lanzarote, he devoted his last 25 years to creating and extending the tourist attractions of the island. As visitors to Lanzarote will know, Manrique created a series of fascinating environments that celebrate its unique landscape: from show caverns and blowholes to houses, gardens and many prominent sculptures and "wind toys."

⬆ *Manrique's building works on the island exploit its many indigenous textures. A volcanic rock wall, the ubiquitous cactus and brilliant tile mosaics are brought together as elements of an abstract composition at the Cesar Manrique Foundation (once his home), Teguise, Lanzarote. The wind toy (top) is just one of Manrique's many inventive creations. This eye-catching landmark has shining metal "cups" to catch the island's steady breeze, sending the concentric circles and fans spinning in opposite directions.*

◀◀ *A pavement at the Museum of Modern Art, Arrecife, Lanzarote. This sensuous texture was created by the artist César Manrique. He has used pebbles from local beaches in an entirely original way, exploiting their natural shapes and displaying their beauty. This pebblework associates happily with modern architecture, the dramatic sea view, exotic plants and modern sculpture.*

FRANCE

JEAN COCTEAU (1889–1963)

"Surprise Me!"

A flamboyant member of 20th-century French avant-garde artistic circles, Jean Cocteau achieved fame in many spheres: as a poet and novelist, as a playwright and set-designer for theater and ballet, as a maker of surrealist films and, not least, as a painter. Towards the end of his life, the southern town of Menton offered him the chance to create the Musée Cocteau within

▶ *A portrait of Orpheus, the mythological hero of Cocteau's most famous film, is drawn in a few bold lines: a modern abstract style that yet has the power to evoke the character and his myth. The mosaic, 6 ft x 5 ft (182 cm x 152 cm), is fixed to the wall at the entrance and greets you, like Cocteau's guiding spirit.*

a 17th-century fort. Here he turned his versatile mind to the creation of an environment fit to house his paintings and drawings; supervising the restoration and designing all the showcases and floors. His pebble mosaic designs both inside and outside the building correspond in character and content to the drawings, tapestries and ceramics within. For Cocteau, pebble mosaic was a useful local craft that allowed him to integrate his personal style into the very fabric of the building, developing themes on walls and floors. He used it as a new kind of painting medium.

🔺 *"Bacchus," another of Cocteau's repertoire of mythological characters, is placed beneath the arches of the modern facade of the Musée Cocteau. The large-scale drawing, transformed into black and white pebblework, blends well with the architectural stonework and stamps a strong identity on the building.*

🔹 *My own drawing of the "Salamander" design from the pebble mosaic inside the Musée Cocteau.*

TURKEY

Pebble mosaic is an indispensable component of the traditional style of Turkish architecture, and still highly valued today. The characteristic Ottoman decorative patterns adapt perfectly to pebble mosaic and, like all Mediterranean mosaics, are made here with small same-sized pebbles.

The principal exponents in Turkey are Sinan Şensoy and Mehmet Işikli. Working together for 15 years, they began work on restoration projects and perfected their own method of in-situ construction. The strong tradition of pebble mosaic floors in the great mansions of the Ottoman Empire, and even in modest traditional houses in historic areas of cities, created a big demand for their work, restoring and constructing new floors in the traditional style.

These two Turkish experts think nothing of undertaking very large projects of between 5000–11,000 sq ft (approximately 500–1000 sq m) with teams of trained workers. Since 2004 they have separated into independent businesses: Sinan, based in Istanbul, retains the name Matusan; and Mehmet runs his own operation as Meandr Handcraft in Antalya. Both continue to make stunning mosaics on a large scale with impeccable workmanship.

SINAN ŞENSOY, MATUSAN

Matusan is in great demand for the embellishment of large mansions lining the Bosphorus, and similar opulent houses throughout Turkey. Drawing upon traditional pebblework patterns, and also adapting motifs and patterns from Turkish ceramics, metalwork, stonecarving and carpets, Matusan adapts the various design elements to suit each particular site. They have become adept in the use of computer technology to draw-up detailed proposals, and to generate stencils for the pebblework.

Sinan's business acumen has led him to develop new lines for export: both "vertical" and "flat pebble" products, in which pebbles are cut or sliced and glued onto a mesh, enabling a whole mosaic to be shipped abroad with minimum weight.

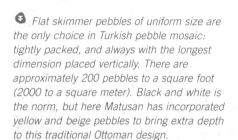

Flat skimmer pebbles of uniform size are the only choice in Turkish pebble mosaic: tightly packed, and always with the longest dimension placed vertically. There are approximately 200 pebbles to a square foot (2000 to a square meter). Black and white is the norm, but here Matusan has incorporated yellow and beige pebbles to bring extra depth to this traditional Ottoman design.

In the last few years, Matusan has developed new motifs and arrangements tailored to suit each particular site. This sunken garden at a mansion in Bursa features Ancient Greek acanthus motifs flanked by contemporary leafy fronds, bordered with a Roman twist pattern.

➤ Matusan's expertise in developing and supplying stone is producing beautiful effects such as this intriguing combination of large-scale motifs cut in smooth marble with impeccable beige pebblework; adding an original touch to this elegant balcony in Istanbul.

⬢ A splendid setting on the Bosphorus for pebble mosaic on a large-scale. This is a typical Matusan project using traditional interlacing patterns and adapting the design to flank the waterside.

⬢ Traditional designs, adapted to the location, make a glamorous landing-stage on the Bosphorus, Istanbul.

◀ An impressive achievement: traditional Seljuk designs in the hauntingly austere garden of a restored mansion overlooking the Bosphorus.

Supplying architectural stonework has always been a part of Matusan's enterprise, and recent work shows impressive expertise in creating a seamlessly integrated style in which the granite and marble surfaces of the surrounding paving are tailored into the overall design along with the pebblework.

For more on Matusan technique see page 36 in chapter 2.

MEHMET IŞIKLI, MEANDR HANDCRAFT

Mehmet has been making pebble mosaics since 1989, and has played an important part in reviving the art in the south of Turkey; restoring old mosaics in his home town of Antalya and producing new designs for the expanding tourist industry on the coast. An artist with many talents, he has created paintings and sculpture for these environments, in addition to his mosaics.

His pebble mosaic designs highlight his mastery of traditional Ottoman patterns. He also shows a playful willingness to experiment with the medium, using his artistic skills to invent new imagery and adapt designs from many sources.

⊗ *Pebble mosaics are in demand for the décor of the developing holiday industry in southern Turkey. Designed by Mehmet Işikli, this impressive piazza at the Atlantis Holiday Village, Bebek, is 115 ft (35 m) in diameter. Sun, wave and shell motifs are integrated with granite paving in a very pleasing way. It is called "Anatolian Civilisation," with the stone sculptures representing different periods of historical development. "Atlantis" is in the center.*

◆ A pebble mosaic team at work in Antalya. Marble paving around a large pool is infilled with panels of pebblework. It's hot: the sunshade hats and mats are necessary! Note the bowls of carefully selected pebbles, the plywood stencils, and the wooden batten ready for tamping down the pebbles as each section is completed. In the shade, Mehmet keeps a sharp eye on the process.

◆ The cheerfulness of a vacation location in southern Turkey. Mehmet's daughter, Canay, is a landscape architect, and designed the whole scheme for this restaurant based on the theme of water. The bar is in the shape of a ship, complete with canvas sails, and the pebble mosaic is a flowing design of whirlpools. The father and daughter team even designed the restaurant's logo and arranged the décor to complete the picture.

◆ Mehmet's exploration of ceramics has influenced an impressive scheme at Belek in Antalya. Blue ceramic tiles are a striking element in the design, contrasting strongly with the black and cream pebbles. Those who know Turkey will appreciate the wonderful tilework in mosques and palaces with their predominant shades of blue. This modern design fuses these influences from history and tradition, combining pebbles and tiles in exciting new patterns.

Pebble mosaics for interiors

Views inside the Minyon Hotel in old Antalya. Ottoman motifs at the entrances and foot of the stairwell combine with borders and geometric patterns to create an authentic look to this restored traditional house.

The elegant lobby of the Perissia Hotel, Side. This traditional Seljuk design in black and white pebbles (with tiny touches of red pebbles in the wavy flower border) is set into a floor of polished, beige-colored granite. It creates a nostalgic atmosphere of fine Turkish craftsmanship within a modern interior. The hotel maintains it beautifully using a vacuum cleaner and occasional washing.

Keeping interior pebble mosaics clean

1. Vacuum cleaning to remove dust between the pebbles.
2. Washing with detergent. Over time, the acids in the detergent give a natural polish to the pebbles.
3. In some situations Matusan applies a "wet look" treatment to accentuate the colors of the pebbles. Bellinzoni and Fila are two Italian brands. The treatment is applied in two stages, 24 hours apart. It should never be used for white pebbles because it deepens the color to a beige or dirty yellow.

FABRIZIO CHIOSTRINI

"There are aesthetic references to the past but, in real terms, the technique is absolutely modern and contemporary."

Intertwined snakes in the Palazzo della Ragione, Milan. They have an interesting bas-relief quality, their rounded contours projecting approximately 1 in (2.5 cm) above the surrounding surface. Each is delineated by strips of brass that are fixed to the base before commencement of pebblework—a technique used in modern terrazzo, and also suggested by the use of lead strips in the ancient Greek mosaics at Pella.

It's encouraging to find that the art of pebble mosaic is still alive in Italy, the home of the Renaissance, where so many great 16th and 17th-century gardens were enlivened by their presence. Fabrizio Chiostrini is a contemporary artist making stunningly original designs and interpreting them in pebble and rock for maximum expression. Nothing is definitive; the craft is adapted to each environment.

Born in Florence in 1965, Fabrizio works in mosaic and other decorative arts throughout Italy. He works in public spaces and private villas, sometimes alone, sometimes together with other artists, and occasionally forms a team of craftsmen to accomplish larger projects.

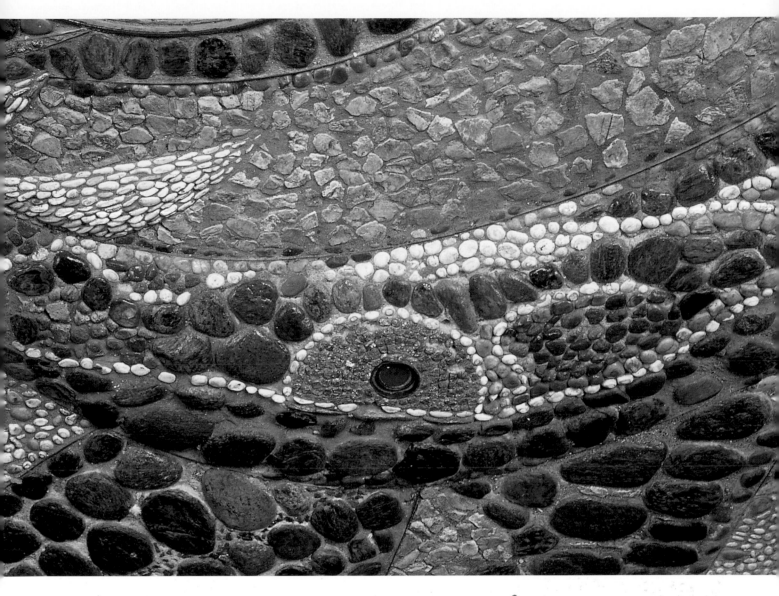

⬆ *The materials used are pebbles and rock fragments from quarries. Large rounded pieces of greenish black granite contrast with angular red rock fragments and small white pebbles. The snake's eye is formed from red glass and a silver-like material that Fabrizio describes as "industrial stone." Note the sharp lines formed by the brass strips.*

 Exciting textures are made with different colors of rock fragments embedded in a special mortar over a metal and concrete structure. It is a similar technique to that used in Renaissance sunken gardens, like the Villa Gamberaia near Florence, and carried out here with great flair.

◀ *A fascinating sculptural garden cascade at Giardino dell'Orticultura, Florence. Fabrizio says, "In the beginning, the idea started from Gaudi (his mosaic in the Parc Guell, Barcelona), but afterwards we took another direction, especially with the materials."*

The cascade begins at the top of a hill commanding a fine view over Florence. A circular pool contains a pillar-fountain with the dragon's tail twisting around it. Its body forms a sculptural channel descending two flights of steps, culminating in this massive head, water pouring from its jaws into the pool below. It's reminiscent of the grand architectural conceits of the Renaissance. Fabrizio has taken the concept and transformed it into an entertaining theatrical set piece for a public park. It's a very large piece of landscape work: the pool, the dragon sculpture, the steps and the "Tree of Life" staircase; and yet Fabrizio speaks of it calmly: "I worked with four people, and we finished it all in six months."

▶ *These steps, either side of the great dragon, are carefully designed with flamelike forms spreading from one step to the next.*

◀ This long flight of 47 steps, separate from the dragon staircase, is Fabrizio's version of the Tree of Life. Every step is different. It begins with 12 steps of roots; they turn into a massive trunk that finally becomes delicate stylized branches, topped off, on the last step, with a sun design.

▶ The "Tree of Life" steps seen from the top.

◆ Each step is made with a different but continuous design. Red, white and black stones (some natural, some "tumbled") contrast well to make an attractive modern design.

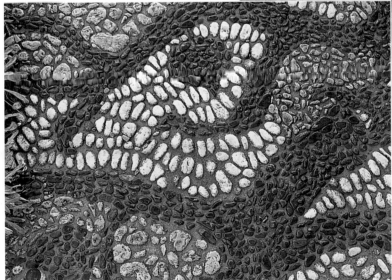

LORNA JORDAN

"The Grotto" by Lorna Jordan, the Waterworks Garden, Renton, Washington. Tendrils, growing from a seedpod, climb and penetrate the walls of the cavelike structure. The materials are marble and granite, gathered as scrap from other installations, or bought from stone suppliers. They were sorted for size and used in angular fragments, or tumbled to make rounded shapes that were used alongside Mexican beach pebbles.

The opposite view of the grotto. Plants are establishing themselves in the organic forms of the mosaic wall. Trickling water reminds the visitor of the ongoing water filtration process and invites contemplation of the forces of nature at work in the garden.

Lorna describes herself as an environmental artist, working to create contemporary spaces that "blur the boundaries between sculpture, ecology, architecture, planning and theater." She lives in Seattle, Washington, a city well known for promoting the concept of art in public places—where large budgets have funded artworks ranging from specially designed manhole-covers to a decorated bus tunnel. But no artist has tackled real social and environmental issues quite like Lorna when she engaged with the floodwater treatment plant at Renton, Washington. She managed to convince the entrenched Public Works Department to give her the power and the means to redesign the essential "dirty water" installation and incorporate it imaginatively into a public garden. Hers is a holistic approach to water purification, using organic methods and creating sculptural "rooms" to educate and entertain visitors.

Pebble mosaic forms only a small part of her overall concept, but is richly used in "The Grotto," one part of the Waterworks Garden. Pebbles and stone interpret the process of filtration and the organic patterns created by particles of the residue. Inspiration came from the 16th-century Italian garden at Bomarzo, described by Lorna as "a Disneyland of the Renaissance." Her garden rooms are informed by a similar kind of themed fantasy. Her grotto theme is a burgeoning seedpod, its tendrils creeping up the cavelike walls. A product called Shotcrete was used to form the organically shaped walls and the mosaic was applied directly onto its surface using a special mortar with latex additive.

Lorna describes the process of making the grotto mosaics: "I worked with Rhodes Masonry to implement the design over a period of about three months. It was the middle of winter, so we had to build a tent over the grotto. I sorted all the stones while they tumbled the marble and granite. Some of the design I pre-conceived, while the rest I drew on the concrete with chalk."

CHRISTINE DESMOND

⏭ *A portrait in pebbles, opposite, is impressive in its precision. The mosaic has been fabricated using the difficult precast technique, where it's so easy for a small pebble to slip slightly out of alignment and make the subject look cross-eyed or gap-toothed. But Christine has a sureness of touch that overcomes these pitfalls.*

⏭ *A mosaic entitled "Theodora." Christine says, "I made Theodora soon after a trip to Ravenna. Her face is based on the original Theodora, but I wanted to give her a more ruthless expression and an original background."*

It always amazes me how mosaicists, all working in the same medium of pebble mosaic, come up with such diverse approaches, and use the medium in such personal and completely different ways. Christine Desmond is an artist who fell in love with the pebblework of Spain, Portugal and Italy and began making mosaics for private gardens in California. A qualified architect, she prefers the satisfaction of working as an artist in metalwork, wooden furniture and garden design. Her work is now dominated by pebble mosaics. She uses pebbles like a painter, acutely aware of each shade, endlessly sorting and selecting to find the right tones for a precise effect.

⏭ *Christine describes the theme: "It all started with Virginia's request for 'a maze that ends with a portrait of my crazy husband.'" A humorous zany design is combined with realistic portraits. Beautiful colors and subtle modeling; a full-on Californian dream!*

JEFFREY BALE

"My work, as a result of the environments that have influenced me, tends to be very organic, or cosmological or totemic."

Jeffrey Bale is outstanding both as a creative artist and for his direct-action approach to gardening and pebble mosaic. Trained as a landscape architect, his first job lasted just 20 minutes in the office, after which point he walked out and began hands-on work in gardens. As he rapidly gained practical experience his creative vision began to emerge, considering gardens as an entirety: the walls and plants, the sculpture, and the role of the garden as a place of contemplation and spiritual refreshment. Later, a visit to Andalusia in Spain, whose gardens are redolent with just such ideas, brought him into contact with the quiet beauty of pebble mosaics.

But Spain was not the real beginning of Jeffrey's fascination with the raw material of the earth. Earlier in life, he had inherited from his geologist grandparents a precious hoard of rocks, and it was thus that he began his love affair with stone in all its variety, from rocks to pebbles. It's fortunate that Oregon and nearby Montana are rich geological regions, revealing a wealth of colored stones for those, like Jeffrey, who are diligent enough to seek them out and spend the time collecting them and sorting them.

Inspiration comes from the rocks themselves: not only those to hand in his own collections, but also those he finds on his world-wide travels. Each winter he takes off on a four-month trip, exploring warmer countries, and he returns with fresh knowledge of different rocks and sculpture, and also patterns and design ideas from as far afield as Asia, Europe and South America.

⬆ A patio representing the thirteen full moons of a year. The spirals have shiny marbles embedded at their centers and, characteristic of Jeffrey's style, the large irregular paving stones are considered for their shape and fit, and enclose yet more small pebbled areas.

"I'm watching you..." Arriving at Jeffrey's ⬇ home in Portland, his eyes are there to greet you and to protect the entrance. One of the big advantages of working on site is the freedom to build using large and small rocks, mixing them with small pebbles and different shapes to make great contrasts. Jeffrey builds walls and steps in the same way. It looks as if he's made it up as he goes along, but of course there is a well-planned idea behind it all.

⬆ *Here's a Western Rattlesnake, 33 ft (10 m) long, lending its wonderful wiggly pattern to this path. Jeffrey's exuberant jungle-y planting invades the spaces between the mosaics.*

"Much of the work I do incorporates spiritual significance. I have built designs using symbolism, numerology, geographic orientations, cosmic alignments, color theory, Vastu Puranic principles and feng shui. My most profound projects involve working in time and space in relation to cosmic cycles, including solstices and equinoxes.

My goal is to create something incredibly beautiful, which in itself is inspirational, and the intention incorporated in the process imbues the mosaic with the power to trigger consciousness in the viewer."

Jeffrey's method of making pebbleworks directly into wet mortar on site is one that he has personally developed, and clearly one that works well for him. I am sure that he has many little "tricks" and habits by which he ensures the soundness and durability of his work.

A summary of Jeffrey's method

A good deal of time is spent in sorting the pebbles in advance: not only for color, but for a good top surface. Particular attention is paid to pre-arranging the larger rocks, making sure that they will fit well and look good. He also makes a drawing of the design and has a clear concept of what is to be achieved. The site is prepared with a solid base, and wooden battens (or forms) are fixed to produce the final finished level. Because of the need to work quickly into wet mortar, good organisation is paramount. Shade or overcast conditions are required, and even then working time is limited to about 20 minutes, after which the batch starts to set. Working on a small area of 3–4 sq ft (approximately 1/3 sq m), mortar is mixed to the consistency of stiff pudding and spread approximately 3 in (7.5 cm) deep, but leaving about 2 in (5 cm) of depth below the finished level. Pebbles are pushed into this, with some scooping out necessary for the larger rocks, packing everything well into the mortar. Once a patch is complete, a board of strong plywood is placed over the work and trodden down by Jeffrey (a ritual dance perhaps?), forcing the pebbles evenly down into the mortar until their tops are level with the battens. Any surplus mortar is then trimmed and sprayed away, and the whole left to cure.

For a more detailed description of Jeffrey's method see his articles in the bibliography.

A parking strip gets a new face with a colorful pebble mosaic in a Miróesque abstract pattern. Jeffrey has just finished washing off the stones; you can see the edge battens still in place, held by pegs. These will be removed later and the gaps filled. Note the flat-topped stones with many different shapes fitted tightly together.

Inspiration for this mosaic derived from the work of Joan Miró. This was commissioned by clients who loved Barcelona, and were passionate about Miró, and the design is a loose interpretation of certain elements from his paintings. Influenced by Miró's surreal approach, Jeffrey takes the lines of pebbles up and over the wall and molds them into the rounded rocks. The colorful background stones are handpicked from "drainage rock" sourced in Montana.

One of the influences on Jeffrey's art is the Persian/Moghul style of rugs and textiles. Here's just one of many "carpets" that Jeffrey has made.

KEVIN CARMAN

Kevin hails from Sarasota, Florida, but works throughout the U.S. A stone mason by trade, an artist by calling, he made elaborate tile mosaics before beginning his work with pebbles. He hand-collects his material, "mostly fossilized bones with the most beautiful semi-polished finishes. I like the idea of incorporating little bits and pieces of our planet's history, even if no-one else sees this."

The mosaics are made by the direct technique (right way up), usually in-situ. Kevin is also experimenting with techniques borrowed from commercial tiles, sometimes cutting stones to a particular depth and applying them to a mesh; thus allowing him to make the mosaic in his studio, and transfer it to site for installation. There is no threat of frost in the sunny southern states, but for security Kevin applies a penetrating sealer to counteract possible damage to softer stones by water absorption and evaporation.

A large mosaic in the forecourt of a large house in Bradenton, Florida. In response to the client's request for a "nature scene," Mark produced this image of a heron set against the burning sun with a second heron also standing on a driftwood tree, silhouetted against a vast expanse of earth.
Concentric circles of long pebbles have created a wonderful effect of shimmering sunlight. Long, thin, feather-like pebbles on the two herons contrast with the flat-topped browns and the small round blacks used for the earth.

◀ Super-thin hand-collected pebbles make a sharp silhouette for this heron, and an almost micro-technique is used for the beak. The large flat-topped background makes a great contrast in texture.

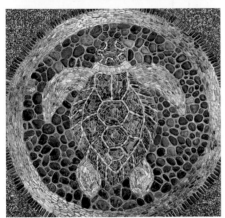

◀ A mosaic for the base of a swimming pool. Pebbles were cut in the studio to a depth of $^{3}/4$ in (18 mm) and fixed to a strong fiberglass mesh using contact adhesive. The finished mosaic was installed by spreading underwater-grade "Thinset" to fix the panels, and grouting with buff-colored cement mortar.

◀ A close-up view of the cut pebbles glued to the mesh before installation on the base of the swimming pool.

▶ "Star Walkway" is the entrance to a house in Atlanta, Georgia. The spindly star-shapes combine well with the irregular stone stabs and the whole design resonates visually with the spiderwebs on the iron gates.

MARK KRETZMEIER

Mark's base is Portland, Oregon. He has always been an artist, working in different media, but constantly interested in placing his creations into an integrated environment. So it's no surprise that he has found, in pebble mosaics, an answer to his desire to make functional art. He enjoys working directly in-situ and achieves a degree of expressive detail remarkable for this technique. His artistry is apparent in the precise drawings that precede the making, and in the lovely colors he manages to source and assemble for each project.

The Jacksonville Zoo Mosaic, Florida. Mark describes the experience of making this in-situ mosaic as a steep learning curve. It was larger than his previous mosaics, 28 ft (8.5 m) in diameter, and was made on site in Florida, 3000 miles (4830 km) from his base in Oregon. In order to divide up the mosaic into manageable sections, he used 3-in (7.5 cm) strips of fiberglass to form each "wave." The animal and wave designs were completed first, and then he tackled the background sections, using strips of wood to separate each one and using slightly bigger rocks and minimal design elements, so the job went twice as fast.

It's worth taking a long look at this beautiful design. What makes it special? Firstly, the mosaic is nicely integrated, "designed-in" to the surrounding landscape. The central fountain makes a lively focus, drawing the eye towards the water. The mosaic design takes the wave shape and plays with it, back and forth, repeating it around the circle. Having set up this strong overall structure, Mark has then lavished attention on the detailed studies of fish and sea-creatures, snakes and bugs which provide plenty of up-close interest and entertainment for visitors to the zoo.

Mark Kretzmeier's drawing for the Florida Zoo mosaic. Here's what he says about the process of translating the original concept into pebble mosaic reality: "The design was months in the planning, with multiple voices making their input. In the original drawing I put in more animals and different plants, but during the planning meeting I was a little offended because they wanted less animals and plants. Now I'm so glad because it saved so much detailed work, and I believe that the final mosaic would have looked much too busy. I had planned on making a full-scale copy of the drawing, but I ended up sketching just the animals and sort of free-styling the border and background."

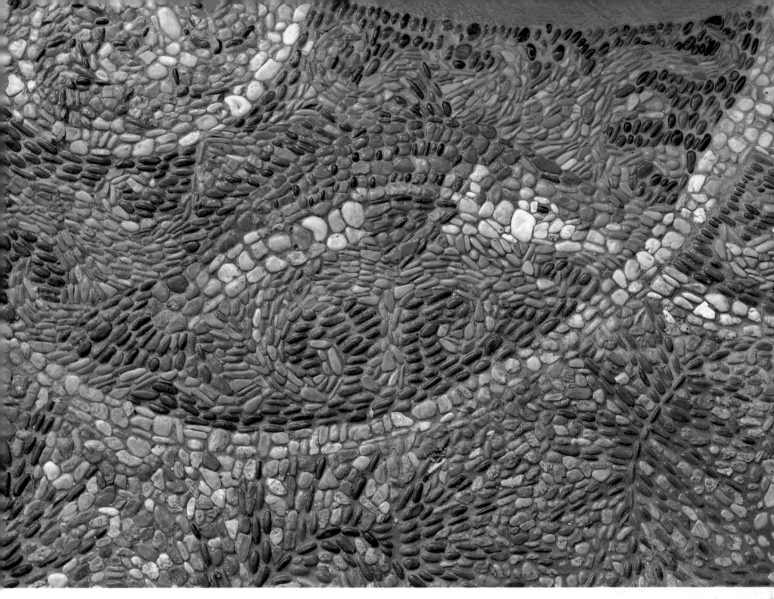

⬆ Mark has used all the shades from yellow to brown stones to emphasize the shape of this fish, while the square-shaped pebbles lend a scaly look. It stands out handsomely against the swirling green and black long pebbles of the waves, which in turn contrast with the rich yellow background and attractive palm like fronds.

⬆ A small mosaic set into existing paving. Prettily detailed flowers and leaves owe their clarity to the precise drawing that preceded this work. I like the way he's used a herringbone pattern in the leaves, and alternating chips of black and white to suggest the detail of the flower center.

⬆ I'm rarely impressed by wall mosaics of pebbles, but here's an exception. What a satisfying effect! Mark has covered the whole wall of this house on Lopez Island with flowing pebble lines like geological strata, or waves from the nearby river where he collected many of the stones. Using "Thinset" he worked up from the bottom, layer above layer.

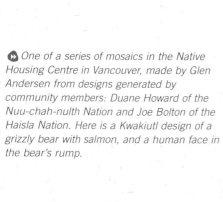

CANADA

GLEN ANDERSEN

"Part of the reason we are attracted to the simple earthiness of pebble mosaics is that we wander through largely de-natured landscapes, depersonalized environments where the origins of materials are unknown. Eventually we stop wondering, and we lose emotional connection with the spirit of this place. These mosaics are conversation starters. Conversations can lead to discussions, debates, revolutions or simply new acquaintants. Mosaics are like communities: each individual piece is essential to the larger picture."

Since the first edition of this book, Glen's pebble mosaics have developed and matured. He now undertakes large commissions in the public arena and private gardens in addition to his commitment to community projects, where he works energetically with participants to secure a successful and permanent outcome. Most of his new mosaics are now pre-cast; his designs continuing to respond to the spirit of place and those who live there.

⬆ *A study called "Surrey Church Window," one of 17 similar pieces based on gothic rose windows built into an architectural scheme with pool and sculptures. Lots of rose quartz and glass make it sparkle in the sunshine.*

⏩ *One of a series of mosaics in the Native Housing Centre in Vancouver, made by Glen Andersen from designs generated by community members: Duane Howard of the Nuu-chah-nulth Nation and Joe Bolton of the Haisla Nation. Here is a Kwakiutl design of a grizzly bear with salmon, and a human face in the bear's rump.*

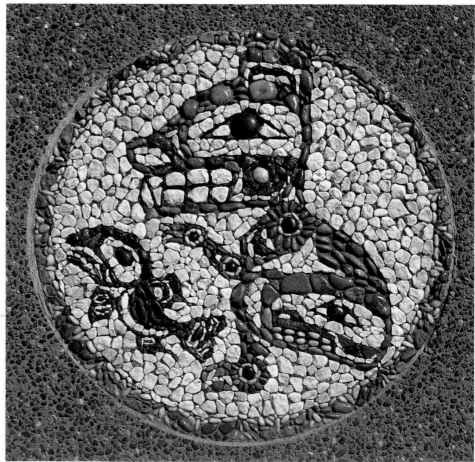

▶ In this mosaic a "Dry Pond" flows between brick walls and spills out on to the four-square brick paved yard. An open-minded client welcomed Glen's creative flair and gave him carte blanche with the design: a big swirl of "water" caught in mid-flow, and filled with many small water-creatures.

◆ An extravagant, action-packed theater of water: not just a swirl, but a waterfall with eddying pools, spills, ripples, waves and a whirlpool. Glen packs in the detail and fills the crannies with turtles and fish and frogs.

Two views of Jennifer Roper's country garden in Northumberland, U.K. Inspiration came from the chorus of a folk song: "The oak and the ash and the bonny rowan tree / They all flourish at home in the north countree." The large simple leaves of oak and ash are made with local river stones. They are selected for their interesting shapes and their smoothness, and then fitted together with great care. A refreshing example of beautiful pebble paths made by a determined individual without reference to any rules or precedents, and entirely for her own private pleasure!

UNITED KINGDOM

The tradition of "cobbling" in the U.K. is still very strong, and an increased interest in conservation has led to some good new work in historic towns and villages. Most of it is plain and utilitarian, but it is good to see that "cobbles" are valued again, even fashionable, after so many years of neglect and destruction. Meanwhile, the creative possibilities of pebbles and other forms of stone have been taken up with enthusiasm by both gardeners and artists.

JENNIFER ROPER

Jennifer is a passionate gardener who has created a beautiful cottage-garden in her home village in Northumberland. Entirely on her own initiative, and following no models either from the U.K. or elsewhere, she has made decorative pebble mosaic paths that wind through densely planted flower borders.

Jennifer began work because she wanted to improve upon the existing unpleasant gravel paths in her garden. The local river furnished an abundance of rough glacial stones in an interesting variety of colors. She began collecting them and, over a long period, built up sufficient stocks to begin her project. At her own pace, and following her own intuition, she made the pebbleworks over several seasons.

Cobbled yards and streets are common in her area, and Jennifer's cobbled paths follow this style, but with care and taste she has achieved unique effects. The stones are large and are selected to fit together snugly, forming simple motifs that contrast delightfully with the rich green plants that surround them.

JOEL BAKER AND CHARLIE MONRO

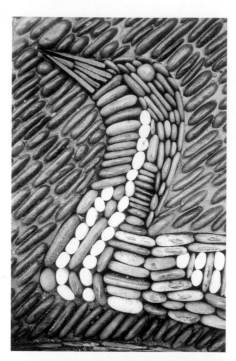

A black-throated diver designed and made by Charlie Monro. Exact placing of the bright yellow eye, and the way the pebbles are arranged on the head and throat give a delightful character to this little bird.

Extending along an awkward steep bank, "The Shoal" captures the moment when a big fish startles a school of smaller fish.

Designed and made by Joel Baker, assisted by Jym Brannah, this mosaic is the centerpiece of a garden mosaic entitled "The Shoal." Expert grading and selection of pebbles makes a lovely diminishing effect in the background and enlivens the movement of the fish. Joel contracted a glass artist to make special effects: the eye was made in ceramic stoneware with a glass pupil, and the "bubbles" are glass that has been cast into cylinder-shaped pebbles.

This Scottish duo (formerly known as Naturescape) continue to make impressive mosaics in the United Kingdom, collaborating on many projects, but also working independently. Originally their strength lay in their in-situ works, made outdoors in all weathers; but recently they have been experimenting with an in-studio pre-cast method based on the "right-way-up" technique. They have developed this because they love to feel and "see" the rhythms of the pebbles as they work.

Joel has described the method as follows: 4 in (10 cm) deep molds with integral plywood bases are filled with an initial 1 in (2.5 cm) layer of sand and grit, and a second 1¾ in (4.5 cm) layer of the usual dry mix (which, when tamped down hard, compresses to 1 in [2.5 cm]). Pebbles are pushed in vertically, their tops tamped down to half an inch (1.2 cm) above the frame of the mold, using strips of ply between the frame and the tamping bar. Then the mold is sprayed with water, setting-off the dry mix layer. A non-shrink grout is poured over and the pebbles are cleaned to leave half an inch (1.2 cm) exposed. After 3–4 days the whole thing is turned over (with extreme care), the plywood base is removed and the sand and gravel layer is brushed and blown away. The enclosing mold still remaining, the back is now filled with a non-shrink grout and gravel mix to create a final slab thickness of around 3 in (7.5 cm). Joel comments that these slabs are strong and withstand the stresses of transportation and installation well.

This is a method reminiscent of the Ernst Bühler technique (see page 180) used by Johannes Vielmetter. It's interesting that Joel and Charlie have found a similar method that suits them.

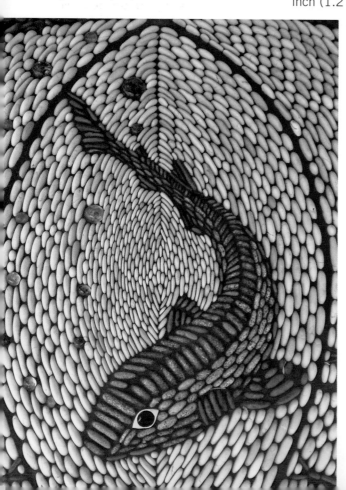

⬤ An interesting treatment of a traditional Celtic Cross, designed by Joel Baker. The mosaic is robustly bordered with granite and raised above the frame of gravel, giving extra definition to the typical cross and circle. The central boss is carved with a Celtic triskele motif. This commission was partly to commemorate their clients' marriage, and also to create a setting for photographers when the house is rented out for weddings.

⬤ Another bird study by Charlie Monro. The very realistic effect is achieved by precise placement of pebbles and a fine choice of textures. It's fascinating to see how each pebble, used in such a decisive manner, is made to "read" as a feather, ear or beak.

⬤ The Celtic triskele is carved from Donegal marble. It fills with water and serves as a bird bath and, for more significant occasions, can be filled with oil and lit.

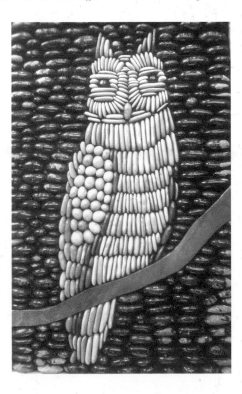

Flat pieces of slate and pebble are arranged as the third eye of the Green Man in a heart-shaped labyrinth pattern.

The "Moon Garden" within the maze, where pebblework forms wave and light patterns spreading from a moon-shaped area.

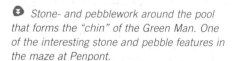

Stone- and pebblework around the pool that forms the "chin" of the Green Man. One of the interesting stone and pebble features in the maze at Penpont.

DAVID EVELEIGH

Penpont is a country house in Wales surrounded by magnificent trees and vistas of rich countryside. Unfortunately, the gardens were neglected for many years until new owners, arriving in 2000, decided not to struggle to restore the old patterns of borders and the labor-intensive walled garden, but to commission something new: a "land art" project. Working to enhance the fine old-established landscape was considered a more appropriate direction for the future of Penpont.

David Eveleigh has for many years been fascinated by the concept of the Green Man, a mythic figure from British and European folklore symbolizing Nature, growth and verdant hedonism. Its symbolism has permeated his work, which ranges widely through performance, environmental art, fire art and, more recently, landscape and garden design. It was in this capacity that David came to Penpont and proposed a maze. His design integrated the maze concept within the face of the Green Man, whose features became sculptural elements in the little garden rooms within the labyrinth.

ROSALIND WATES

Rosalind is an artist who has made mosaics all her life. Whereas others might demur at the difficulties of new techniques, Rosalind seems fearless; wide experimentation has given her a sure touch in her innovative projects in pebble and stone.

Three-dimensional projects in pebble mosaic are rare because the difficulties of construction are so great. Rosalind's "Giant Mackerel" on North Uist, Scotland, is an inspiring example: the result of determined research on the job. She describes the process as follows: "The structure of the mackerel is an aluminium frame bolted to the rock; this is covered with galvanized mesh, which in turn is covered with Powerwall. This latter is a cementitious and resinous render which, incidentally, is used to coat lighthouses, and is tested in seawater. The sculpture is designed to cope with the sea, as several times ab year it is submerged by high tides. The pebbles and shells are embedded using this same Powerwall, and the mussel shells are also coated with a cement hardener to give them extra toughness."

⬆ *A glorious unspoilt site on the remote Scottish island of North Uist provided the opportunity for a 3-D fish sculpture, designed to celebrate the local environment and wildlife using locally found materials. Rosalind found a wealth of colored pebbles on the island: "glorious translucent egg-like washed quartz, shiny black basalt, a range of wonderful grainy cold grays, pinks and yellows, as well as green and brown broken glass and blue mussel shells." The giant fish concept took shape because the sea and fishing are so important to the island. A mackerel was chosen because of its rich patterning. At 16 ft 3 in (5 m) long, the sculpture has the stature of a monument and lies, unadorned, like a giant of its species washed up on the rocky foreshore.*

⬅ *An otter made with different colors of slate, celebrating the wildlife of the area with material from local quarry tips. Having experience of tile and tesserae mosaic techniques, Rosalind Wates assembled the rough fragments into a simple and elegant otter. Located deep in the forest, the mosaic is a surprising encounter on the trail through Grizedale Forest in Cumbria, U.K.*

JANETTE IRELAND

After several years as a highly-valued assistant at the Cobblestone Designs workshop, Janette eventually took the plunge and began working independently, developing her own distinctive style. Her interest in the textures and patterns that can be achieved with pebbles has always been her strength. Now she is making large mosaic commissions in the U.K. and breaking new ground by integrating metal sculpture into her work.

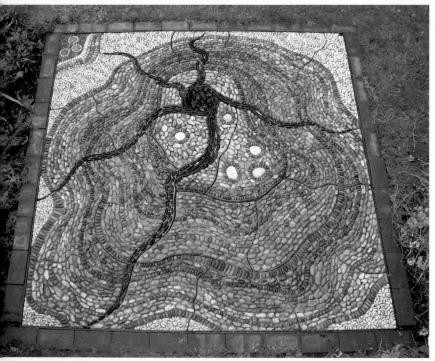

Pebble mosaic and steel sculpture are combined in a collaboration between Janette Ireland and Chris Bramall. The sculpture is a memorial to a historic aqueduct near Preston, United Kingdom. The pebbles represent the water that it once carried, and the sculpture shows half of the aqueduct arch, with the other half physically located nearby. Setting the pebbles securely to flow up and over the Corten steel form required some thoughtful design. A "box" channel was situated inside, with a lip like a picture frame to contain the pebbles. Each side of the sculpture was made separately, the pebbles being placed by the normal method and then grouted to fill the box channel. After this the sculpture was welded together.

Janette's love of textures and patterns can be fully appreciated in this mosaic where gray and brown flints combine with red and black granites and plum and white Chinese pebbles in abstract flowing lines. Originally designed to incorporate a fountain in the center, the mosaic suggests the eddies of water and lines of sediment spreading over flowery ground.

This mosaic was commissioned to celebrate the history of shipbuilding in Barrow, U.K. The launch of a new ship would once have been a regular event here, and the prow of this vessel stands like a large "V," a reminder of the dockyard name of Vickers-Armstrong.

Janette's design shows the launch and brings a champagne-style flourish with red iron-ore-colored pebbles rising like bubbles. Twisting ropes lead to motifs of wheat and barley that were sources of the town's earlier prosperity, in addition to its shipbuilding and steel industries.

COBBLESTONE DESIGNS—My Own Work

The objective of my work has always been to celebrate the spirit of place; to underpin the uniqueness of each location with specially designed hand-made mosaics, reflecting local themes, materials and color. In the past, they have often been designed for town centers and public parks, but in recent years commissions for private gardens have increased, often providing beautiful settings for the mosaics. In spite of their restricted audience, I enjoy the opportunity to dream up extravagant designs, pushing both my own creative thinking and the medium itself into new areas.

My workshop assistants are the many hands that make light work of the larger pebble mosaics. They are Mark Currie, the "ultimate craftsman;" Janette Ireland, who also undertakes her own commissions; Nick Brown and my son, George Howarth.

⬆ *A small mosaic for a private garden 40 x 60 in (1 x 1.5 m) has just enough space for this bird study and a decorative border. The background of radiating black pebbles helps to focus attention on the thrush.*

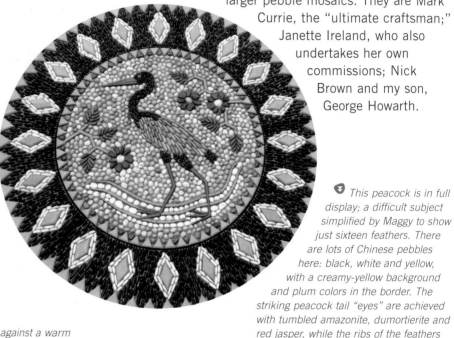

⏩ *This small heron mosaic is a popular design and is made as a limited edition at Cobblestone Designs, called a "readymade." Here there is an added border of cut slate and black pebbles.*

⬇ *Ceramic swallows swoop around a small mosaic against a warm background of mixed granites.*

⬇ *This peacock is in full display; a difficult subject simplified by Maggy to show just sixteen feathers. There are lots of Chinese pebbles here: black, white and yellow, with a creamy-yellow background and plum colors in the border. The striking peacock tail "eyes" are achieved with tumbled amazonite, dumortierite and red jasper, while the ribs of the feathers are white porcelain.*

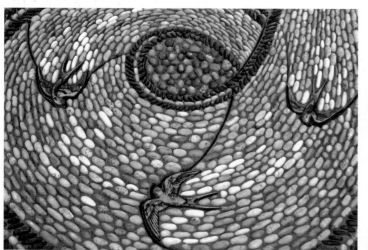

◄ Shading and grading are what it's all about in this mosaic made for the Chelsea Flower Show, U.K. in 2004. Commissioned by Cancer Research UK, the theme was LIFE! The design tosses opposing spirals around a central pool, and makes the pebbles flow in diminishing and expanding lines to express the vibrancy of the "rhythm of life." The pebbles make a three-dimensional effect by shading through light to dark: bright white quartz, not-so-white limestone, grayish limestone, light gray granites, green tumbled slate and finally dense black Chinese pebbles. The mosaic is now permanently installed at In-Ex Garden Center, Goffs Oak, Hertfordshire, U.K.

In Memory of
HUGH GEORGE
Sixth Marquess of
CHOLMONDELEY
MC GCVO
1918-1990

"Shell Mosaic" was made for a large shallow pool at the head of a series of descending pools: an impressive landscape feature with its encircling path. Maggy's interest in shading was applied to give a three-dimensional quality to this giant shell, with its decorative raised border. Some fun here with the pebbles: special jewel-like stones, together with some fossils and rare exotics, were mixed to make a rock-pool-like background for the shell. From here the water flows down a long rill, with formal pools and fountains: a landscaping scheme on a grand scale, at Thenford House, Oxfordshire.

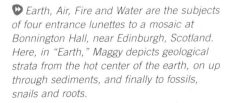

This 14½ ft (5 m) mosaic has a wonderful setting in the landscaped grounds of Cholmondeley Castle in Cheshire, U.K. Made to commemorate the life of Lord Cholmondeley, whose home it was, the design shows aspects of his life depicted in ceramic inserts in the border: military insignia, drums, prize cattle, horses and foxes and pheasants. Maggy simplified and re-drew the central crest in an entertaining style, bringing formal heraldry to life.

Earth, Air, Fire and Water are the subjects of four entrance lunettes to a mosaic at Bonnington Hall, near Edinburgh, Scotland. Here, in "Earth," Maggy depicts geological strata from the hot center of the earth, on up through sediments, and finally to fossils, snails and roots.

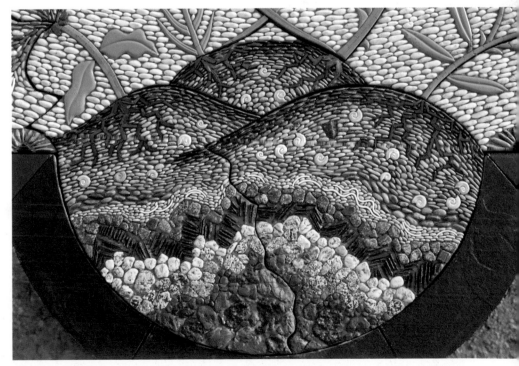

AUSTRALIA

ALAIN & KATE COLFS

⬇ *The Simpson Desert.*

Yet again I am amazed at the wonderful way in which pebblework changes its appearance in different continents, conditioned by different cultures, environment and local materials. Some years ago Alain and Kate Colfs contacted me, sending photos of their "take" on pebblework. They had already spent many years as skilled glassworkers making stained glass mosaics. More recently, they began to undertake "community art" projects, an important part of Australian culture, reaching out to the isolated communities of the interior.

While running a workshop at a small settlement on the edge of the Simpson Desert, it was suggested that use might be made of the locally abundant "gibbers," which are wind-smoothed fragments of chalcedony coated with iron oxide. So began their interest in pebble mosaic: a timely story of an artistic response to local environment and materials.

⬇ *So very different! Local "gibbers," the rich red stones that form the characteristic floor of the Simpson Desert, are used as a unifying background material in these mosaic sections, making up a free-standing "sign" for a new clinic. The images celebrate this special environment: they include duck, emu, dingo, brolga crane, insects, desert flowers and truck tracks in the sand. A terrific effort by the full-complement of 120 inhabitants of Birdsville.*

A big snake sign for a small town of 2500 people; just one of the many imaginative community projects undertaken by Kate and Alain Colfs. Styrofoam letters were glued to the base of the mold made for each section, following the pattern and sitting among the pebbles. After casting, the Styrofoam was removed and replaced with glass mosaic. The supporting steel structure was 21 ft (6.3 m) high. Each section of the mosaic had a ½ in (12 mm) square bar embedded into the concrete at the back, to which mounting bolts were welded for fixing to the steel support.

▶ An inventive cartoon image made in another community project, this time in Tambo, central-west Queensland. Made with an upside-down technique, colored resin is used in an interesting way to create lines around the bird. Rope is glued with PVA to the bird pattern on the base of the mold, which is then completed with the glass detail and pebbles. After the slab has been cast and turned out, the rope is removed. Later, when the mosaic has been cured, the resultant groove is filled with black resin.

◀ Alain says: "For the kangaroo head, we shaped brass strips and brazed them to the required shape, as you would do for terrazzo. This enabled us to separate the colors. We used ivory cement and white sand to give us flexibility with the background coloring and to achieve a better color contrast."

It's a distinctive style, informed by Alain's skills as plumber and builder, and a bold "no worries" attitude to innovation.

▶ The skilfully directed combination of glass mosaic and pebble background has proved a good formula for these Australian community projects. Alain comments: "Most of the materials are available locally, and technical skills are acquired fairly quickly (although mastering the sand depth takes a bit of time and patience). As our designs are done mainly in glass and resin, and we're often working with people of all ages and abilities, we have to accept that the placement of pebbles is not so critical."

When I asked Alain about the possibility of the glass breaking, he responded, "It's very durable underfoot as long as the pieces are not too big. We now recess the glass $1/8$ in (3–4 mm) and then coat it with resin as a precaution."

WENDY CLARKE

Wendy is a landscape architect and garden designer whose philosophy is to realize, for her clients, their dreams of the personal space they would like to inhabit. This frequently takes her into uncharted territory, even close to home. The mosaic she made for her own office building is an interesting combination of pebble, tile and exposed aggregate, which is a popular surface finish in Australia. Exposed aggregate technique relates to pebble mosaic because it presents a way of filling areas and producing a relatively interesting surface, depending on the mix of aggregates and sand that are used. It also relates to terrazzo, where the surface is later ground to a fine, smooth polished finish.

Wendy has combined an exposed aggregate surface with a direct placing of pebbles and tile to great effect. Her mosaics remind me of the early terrazzo floors of 18th-century Venice, but when I mentioned this, she replied: "More terror than terrazzo! Everything had to be accomplished at such a speed; working with the setting time of the concrete and seeding it with pebbles as the mix stiffened." It's a great idea, and very effective in combination with the brightly colored tile mosaic.

An interesting combination of direct pebblework and exposed aggregate by Wendy Clarke. The central sun motif of tiles and pebbles was pre-made, and clear sticky PVC sheet was stuck to the exposed surface to hold it in place for transportation. On site, the concrete was poured in a single visit and Wendy immediately went to work, setting the big pebbles into swirling shapes and then laying the pre-formed mosaic into the concrete as it began to set. The PVC was gently removed and the whole area was tamped to press in the added elements. As the concrete hardened, the surface was washed to reveal the attractive colored aggregate and introduced pebbles. Wendy comments: "I lost a few crucially arranged bits here and there. Next time I'll do it better."

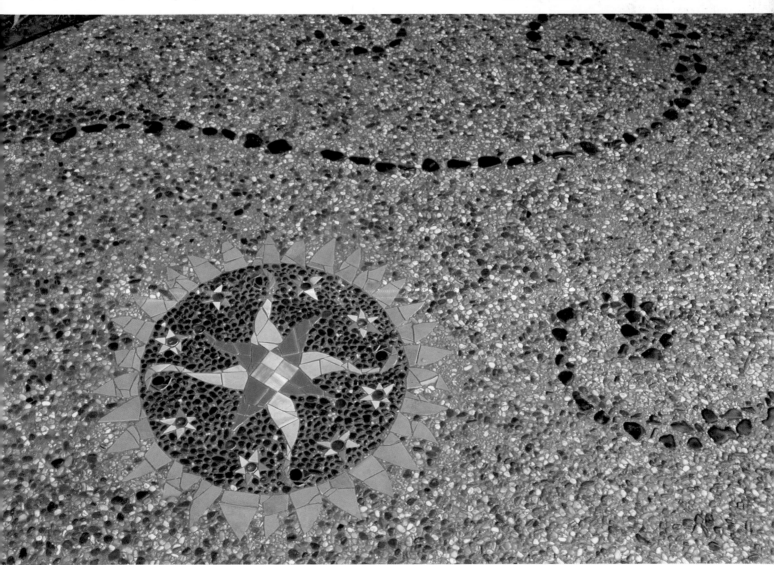

JOHN BOTICA

In a few short years, John has achieved considerable recognition as a pebble mosaic craftsman in his own country and further afield. A former international tennis player and coach, he came to pebblework via tile mosaic, embracing both media with characteristic passion. He is self-taught, having taken the plunge into this difficult medium only four years ago, armed with the first edition of this book and a possible commission in sight. He soon acquired a technical mastery of the pre-cast technique, and rapidly gained experience, making large mosaics in public locations.

He gets very excited about pebbles! Perhaps this is the reason why his style is so remarkable for the sheer perfection of his pebblework, almost to the point of obsession. Each chosen pebble is an exact shape and precisely off-set in each row. The rows are exactly matched, or if John decides to vary the rhythm, that is exactly what he achieves. He has combined this rigorous discipline with a strong and simple approach to design, drawing on the Maori and Polynesian patterns so much a part of New Zealand culture.

A lively black and white mosaic adorns a Sports Center in Auckland. It's called "Kopu," the Maori for "Morning Star."

"When you have seen one pebble mosaic in person you will perceive how single pebbles move, how expressive they are, and how full of texture one pebble mosaic can be. I call it sculpture on the ground."

John has made several pebble mosaics to adorn public parks in Auckland. This one, in Western Park, shows the influence of Maori themes common in New Zealand art. John explains, "The big flower is the frangipani flower, much depicted by Polynesian artists. The trees are Nikau palms, the only native New Zealand palm trees. On the perimeter you see koru: these are wave-swirls that are an integral part of Maori art. A koru is a representation of a newly unfurling fern frond, symbolizing growth, strength and peace."

Even lines of matching pebbles are assembled with John's typical attention to perfect detail. Pebble mosaicists everywhere will appreciate his arduous work in collecting, grading and placing these pebbles to create this fine quality finish.

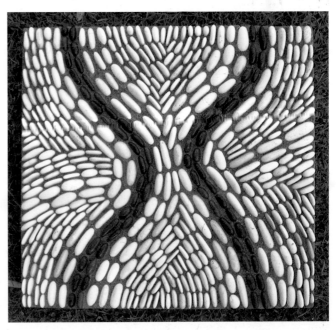

A charming abstract mosaic where the force of the flow of the pebbles appears to "push" the black lines together.

⬆ This mosaic, called "Tree of Life," decorates a children's playground in an area of Auckland that has a rooster as a mascot for its sports teams. Apple trees with chickens scratching underneath are a familiar sight, and so John was asked to design something using these themes, also including a weather vane. He has adopted a very stylized approach, emulating the simplicity of a child's painting. The pebblework is amazingly uniform and even.

⏩ John's compass design is popular with New Zealand's yachting enthusiasts. The traditional pointed star has a 3-D effect.

▶▶ A recent small piece which experiments with different sizes and colors of perfectly-selected pebbles: some from China and Indonesia, and some of John's yellow and gray New Zealand pebbles.

▶ John loves these gray New Zealand pebbles, which he describes as "assuming many shades of green when they are wet." Once again, they are laid in even matching rows, their almost military discipline containing the bold swirling design. Note how the low directional light of the evening sun on the pebblework creates a fascinating effect, like brushed fur.

ULA SIEGERS

Ula Siegers is an artist from Niederkrüchten, near the Dutch border. Her work is reminiscent of traditional German pebblework (like the decorative pavements of Freiburg and Salzburg), although she is unaware of any direct influence. Her inspiration comes from pebbleworks that she discovered on her worldwide travels as a professional orchestral musician. When she first began to decorate her own garden with pebble mosaics she remembers that she had the feeling that "I was a big explorer who had a brilliant idea: collecting pebbles, sorting them and putting them together like pieces of a puzzle." Her art is a response to the characteristic qualities of the pebbles in her hands, rather than a premeditated ordering of units of stone. At present, Ula is making pebble mosaic panels for interior decoration, creating small pieces for walls and floors, paying close attention to fine detail. The pebbles that she uses are smaller than in her previous work. She calls herself "a specialist in miniature pebble mosaic."

❯❯ Astonishing realism! A scarab beetle by Ula Siegers, made as a wall panel. Individual pebbles suggesting particular insect characteristics are assembled with great accuracy. From miniature mosaics she has moved on to the realm of bas-relief, making her images of beetles, crabs, scorpions and ants look even more realistic.

❯❯ Recently, Ula has been using pebbles to make three-dimensional sculptures. Her two pieces of "Kieselfrüchte" (literally Flint-fruit) are lovely objects, only 14 in (35 cm) long, and are made by an ingenious method. The pebbles themselves are the initial inspiration; Ula found some that looked like a big kernel and others like dry pieces of stalk. Using a half-spherical bowl as a form, the outer surface was made using tile cement and textile to hold the pebbles. Later the form was turned over and the interior body of the fruit was made using mortar colored with red Spanish sand into which the kernel and seeds were set.

❯❯ Opposite: Spiral, star, shell-pattern, checkers and linear borders: all mingle in Ula's style. Fifteen years on from making this mosaic she wishes she had paid more attention to technique. "What fascinated me was the great variety of forms in the pebbles that we have. I always used the best-looking side, even if it was the flat one. I shouldn't have done that!" Beginners, note Ula's warning. Always be sure that your technique complements your artistry.

JOHANNES VIELMETTER

Johannes is inspired by rocks and pebbles to make "stone paintings" for walls, rather than floors or pavements. It is what he calls "the poetic quality," the shape, feel and color of each pebble or rock fragment, that determines how he uses it. Each makes its mark and, like a painter, he freely mixes his effects and contrasts, keeping us continually aware of the special qualities of each stone.

Johannes collects his stones throughout the world, from quarries, riverbeds, beaches and deserts. He also buys brightly colored precious stones like lapis, turquoise and amethyst. Sometimes "for reasons of expressiveness" he uses very rough, broken, even quite large chunks of rock that stand out from the picture in relief.

He pays tribute to his old Swiss teacher, Ernst Bühler, who first inspired him and then taught him the techniques of rock painting. (Together they have made a number of works in Biel, Switzerland.) He calls this technique "the indirect setting method."

The Indian portraits (the example on the opposite page is one of many versions) have their origins in a culturally rebellious phase when Johannes sought a new life on an Indian reservation, hoping to settle amongst a community with similar antimaterialistic and antiestablishment ideals. The experiment ended in disillusion, but the images he brought away with him—the Native American faces, the animals and birds—endured and still provide inspiration for his stone mosaics.

⬆ *Among the bright-colored rocks used for this exotic fish are turquoise from Arizona and China, lapis lazuli, dumortierite, blue quartz, amazonite, azurite and purple calcite. Note the contrasting scale of the tiny pieces used for the eye and fins against the size of the colored scales. Then again, the large chunks interspersed with small pebbles in the light-colored background. Contrast, surprise, playfulness with the materials! There is a constant search for special and individual stones to represent a form.*

⬇ *An impressive rock painting by Johannes Vielmetter. A huge variety of stones and pebbles have been assembled to suggest the rich tones of this powerful face. Enjoy the way he uses bulbous pebbles for lips and chin, jagged chunks for hair, tiny kaleidoscopes of color for the pupils of the eyes. Johannes' training as a painter shows in the touches of brilliant green and blue he "mixes" into the deep shadows, intensifying the color and contrast.*

Herons are flapping over their nest of young against a background of reeds and grasses. A myriad subtle effects in color and texture are used to bring this dramatic scene to life, from the delicate shades of water-plants to the strong dark feathering of the birds. A large stone mosaic by Johannes Vielmetter and his teacher and mentor, Ernst Bühler. A complex work measuring 6 ft 7 in x 12 ft (2 m x 3.7 m) on the wall of a rest home in Biel, Switzerland.

A swooping eagle just before the kill. Another source of inspiration from Johannes' time on the Indian reservation. Big pieces of multicolored rock approximate the texture of feathers. An intense red rock adds a flash of color to the wings, and a swirling background of jagged white pebbles suggests the turbulent air around the bird.

The construction technique of Ernst Bühler

Using a wooden board for a base (the same size as the intended picture) and protecting it with plastic, a wooden frame is constructed around it. This frame must be *about* $1/2$ in (1 cm–1.5 cm) higher than the tallest rock to be used. The base of the frame is filled with a moist layer of sand that is deep enough to support the stones and pebbles to be embedded into it to make the rock picture.

Once completed, the picture must be cast. A layer of sticky clay is pressed onto the surface of the rock picture to the level of the frame. This fixes all the rocks and pebbles in place. Then another board, covering the surface of the clay, is screwed on top of the frame. The whole thing is so tightly packed that it can be turned over without any pebbles becoming dislodged. The backing board is unscrewed and taken off together with the plastic sheet. The moist sand must now be carefully removed; an air jet is used for the last particles. The "backside" of the rocks is thus exposed and ready to be cast. For this, several layers are used: first, a wet mortar; then, a special mixture of artificial resin and water; and finally, a concrete mix. Large mosaics are reinforced with steel mesh and rods.

Once this has cured, the mosaic is turned over again and all the clay peeled away and washed off.

NOTE: Recent stone pictures by Johannes Vielmetter can be seen at the garden of the late Ernst Bühler in Switzerland, and also in a large mosaic collection at a nearby old-people's home, Alterswohnheim Büttenberg. Both locations are in 2504 Biel-Bienne, Switzerland. The garden: Meienriedweg 4 is open anytime; the home: Geyisriedweg 63 has a garden and the interior collection can be seen by appointment.

GREECE

YIANNIS LOUKIANOS

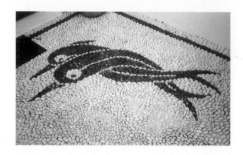

An attractive motif of dolphins in black and white on Milos Island.

Yiannis Loukianos at work on a pebble mosaic.

Yiannis Loukianos is not only a contemporary artist and maker of pebble mosaics, but also an authority on the history and restoration of the traditional pebble mosaics of Greece.

How easy it is to lose the craft skills that distinguish a traditional built environment! After a glorious beginning with the achievements of the Hellenistic period, the art of pebble mosaic was lost in Greece, due to the vicissitudes of successive occupations, and did not re-appear until the late 18th century. Yiannis has been waging a concerted lecturing campaign to encourage the appreciation of this second flowering of pebble mosaic in Greece, particularly in the "pebbled yards" of the Greek islands. He has also completely rebuilt important mosaics that had fallen into disrepair.

The Greek pebble mosaic tradition is of particular interest for its rich variety of patterns, thematic material and motifs. The beginnings can be traced through Ancient Greece to Byzantium, yielding a plethora of symbolic subjects such as the twin-headed eagle that is still popular for the entrance to churches. The Greek and Roman meander and wave scrolls are common; and an Ottoman influence can be seen in some floral patterns. Subjects drawn from everyday life extend the palette: birds, flowers, animals, anchors, ships and stars; myth and superstition bring mermaids and dragons; the image of the cypress tree is widespread, and the lion acts as guardian angel, while the snake is a symbol of goodness.

Yiannis has inherited all this iconography from his native tradition and continues to draw upon his accumulated knowledge to create new designs.

A brief description of the traditional Greek technique for pebble mosaics:

1. Site preparation. For a modern "Rolls-Royce" specification Yiannis recommends three compacted layers of crushed rock, sand and cement to a depth of 10 or even 20 in (25–50 cm); but in traditional practice this is often much less, using a single layer of red earth mixed with quarry sand, soaked with water and then leveled.

2. The pebbles used are of a uniform size, and usually black and white.

3. A layer of soft mortar is spread to a depth of 3/8 in (1 cm) with 2 parts of fine sifted sea-sand to one part of lime. The use of lime allows the mortar more permeability and flexibility than cement.

4. The pebbles are positioned vertically and pushed slightly into the mortar, tightly packed together.

5. When complete, fine sand is thrown over the surface and the whole area is beaten down with a flattening tool, like a mallet with a large square of flat wood attached. This "ironing-out" process stabilizes the work and brings all the pebbles to a flat surface. Subsequently, the excess sand is lightly swept away and the entire surface kept moist.

A pebble mosaic by Yiannis Loukianos in the yard of a house on Milos Island, Greece. This circular motif is one of many variations of the star/sun, this one with 64 rays.

CHINA

SHANGHAI LANDSCAPE ARCHITECTURE DESIGN INSTITUTE (S.L.A.D.I.)

China today is developing its infrastructures at an accelerating pace, opening up to trade with the rest of the world, and eager to develop its economy for the benefit of its huge population. Change and development are everywhere—and nowhere more strikingly than in Pudong, across the Yangtze River from Shanghai, where skyscrapers are built at the rate of one a year in vast landscaped parks.

The S.L.A.D.I. undertakes large projects in these city parks and "scenic spots," such as the Grand View Screening System, as well as building hotels and designing Chinese gardens in other countries. Architecture, landscape, public sculpture, town planning and road building are all encompassed in one organization.

When I met members of S.L.A.D.I., I discovered that they appreciate pebble mosaic for its texture and "atmospheric" character. But I felt that my questions regarding their work were somehow missing the point: I was dwelling too much on details. These modern Chinese professionals are dealing with a far broader picture, using washes of texture in abstract designs on a grand scale. They showed little interest in small "paintings" on the ground. While respecting traditional pebblework, and indeed, well able to recreate it when required, their interest lies in the great wind of change that is blowing through China.

➡️ *The city is densely populated, and people have little or no private space; so the inner-city parks (sometimes constructed beneath vast overpasses) are well used. Exercising for health is a popular pursuit. Early morning sees people running, dancing and practicing tai chi. Here you can see people massaging their feet by walking on a specially made pebble pavement: an old Chinese idea for well-being that was practiced by the Empress Cixi on pavements she had built at the Summer Palace, near Beijing.*

➡️ *Opposite: A view in the Guqi Garden, Shanghai, designed by S.L.A.D.I. The pebble-work covers large areas and here shows the cracked-ice pattern around the Pavilion of Eight Scenes. The foreground motif is one of the eight; they symbolize the magic powers of different "gods": clubs, fans, swords and so on.*

For most projects, construction teams are in charge of the pebblework. The pebbles are pressed vertically into a "damp" concrete mix (too wet and it would spill over the surface of the pebbles); then the surface is brushed off and cleaned up later. Regarding materials, they said, "We use what is available locally." In view of the long distances between one center and another, this makes total sense. Improvising creatively with "what is available" creates the interesting variety that can be seen in Chinese pebblework today.

♻ A monument bearing all the Chinese characters that stand for "long life" (more than 100 of them) is carried on the back of a stone turtle in the Guqi Garden, in Liading district, Shanghai. This is a new garden created under the direction of the S.L.A.D.I. It is designed on traditional lines, creating sculptural monuments and buildings with rockwork and pebble mosaics. Mr. Xia, the garden's director for over 20 years, was proud to show his work. The pattern of the turtle shell is repeated in the pebblework around the sculpture.

♦♦ More of the magic symbols from the Guqi Garden pavements: A magic horn and a decorated sword tied with ribbons. Mixed pebbles, ceramic shards and broken tile delineate the motif, which is set against a background of rough rock fragments.

EMERGING NEW TALENT

It's always exciting to see new artists producing good work in pebble mosaic and beginning to forge new careers for themselves. Here are a few to watch; already they are producing work with a distinctive personal vision and establishing themselves in their own various countries.

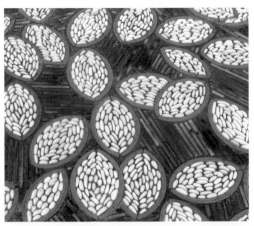

Karen Thompson is an experienced mosaicist in tile and glass whose first foray into pebblework was this impressive 165 sq ft (15 sq m) Chinese-style mosaic in California. Design is second nature to her; it was the technique that she had to master. She pre-cast the "leaves" using ceramic sections of tiles for molds. The contractor provided a very smooth and consistent concrete base, and the rest of the work was done on site, laying out the leaves and filling the interstices with more slices of tile. Made in 2007 in collaboration with BAMO.

Deb Aldo is a garden designer from Connecticut who is exploring many ways of integrating stone and mosaic into landscape settings. She likes to create environments that are tailored to suit the personality of the owner. This garden features a medallion pebble design with classical palmette and scroll motifs, and reflect the clients' interest in classical patterns. Deb repeats the stone, pebble and brick elements in the path and steps beyond, showing how effective well-chosen combinations of pebbles of different sized stones can be on a larger scale.

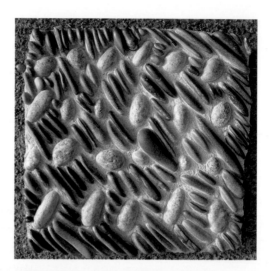

● Laura Stone lives in the small town of Knife River on Lake Superior. Her home is on the shore, so her work is driven by the infinite variety of pebbles to be found outside her door: beautiful colors and unique water-worn shapes. Laura is one of the few who only work with what material they can personally collect. And this makes a great difference: a deeply contemplative quality derived from the hours of collecting and arranging, making each and every stone "special." This is "Smelt Run:" a small mosaic capturing a fleeting moment with a few well-chosen pebbles.

● David Eveleigh brings a holistic approach to his pebble pavements in the U.K. Sourcing and collecting local materials such as these wonderfully-varied river pebbles, he then makes traditional-looking mosaics in a simple modern style. It's a pleasure to see this kind of work that so perfectly inhabits the English country-house style of garden.

● A lovely dragonfly by Sue Rew in the U.K. makes an interesting addition to a garden patio. She has used some green glass cylinders on the body and interesting fiber-optic balls for the eyes, which have an iridescent effect. More glass is used in the shimmering wings: this time it's green glass "nuggets" combined with slate strips for the veins.

◀ *Inci Ümmühan works in Istanbul, Turkey, making stunning wall mosaics. She has made creative use of the new technique of gluing cut pebbles to a mesh. In the "Orlando Tree" Inci has used flat, sliced, cut vertical pebbles and even smalti to make a glamorous wall-piece for an architectural setting.*

◀ *In Holland, Ariane Wachsmuth used a direct technique to make these attractive pillars in a swimming pool complex; arranging the colors spirally in bands like the scales in a long reptile skin. The effect is very tactile, with gleaming white grout emphasising the mosaic pattern of the pebbles.*

◀ *Scottish garden designer, Andrea Scholes, is skilled in the integration of stone, pebbles and plants into a single unified vision. This "Contemplative Garden" uses pink, gray and white pebbles to make a pretty floral design within an encircling wall, while the furniture and planting scheme add contrasting textures to the overall composition.*

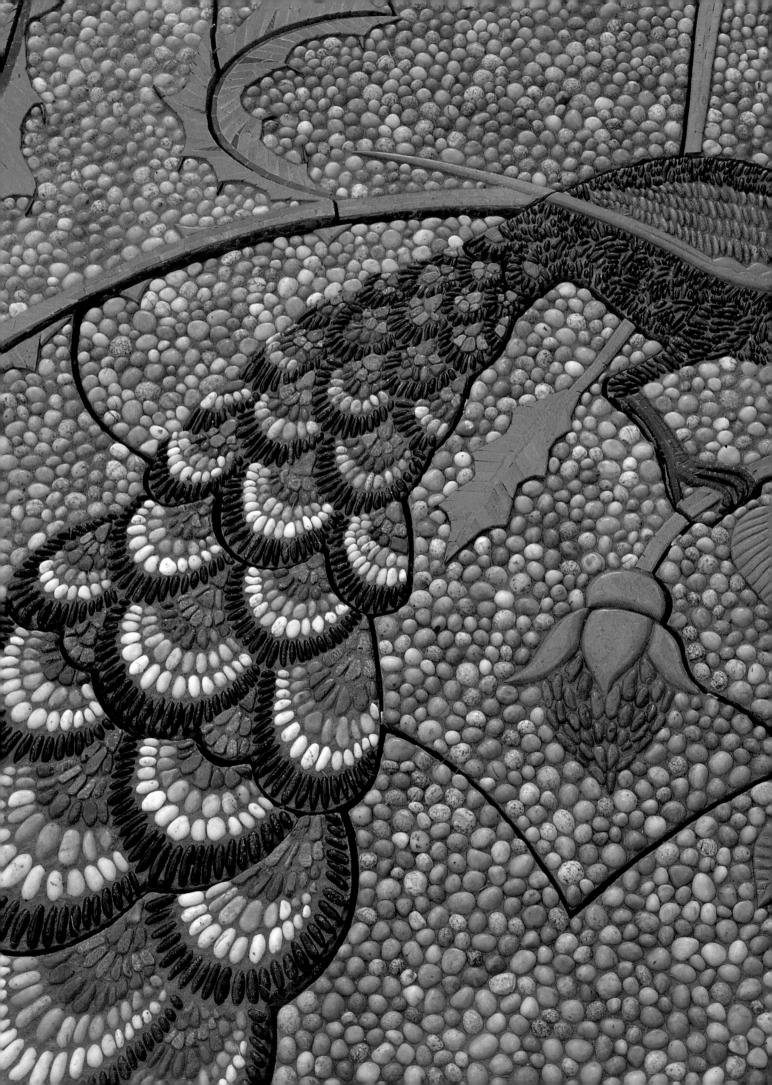

Section **3**

Gazetteer
of Design
Ideas

This final section is intended to give you plenty of ideas for pebble mosaic. All of the themes here have been tried and tested: made into pebble mosaics by others or me, or designed with pebbles in mind. You should find a lot of good starting points, and some extra advice covering other aspects of design such as scale and materials.

Note: To save repetition in the captions, whenever the artist/designer is not stated, the designs and mosaics are by Maggy Howarth and Cobblestone Designs.

ALLOVER PATTERNS

⏩ *Like knotted mesh, this pattern of black and white pebbles echoes the design of the arch and trelliswork, Eva Piges, Rhodes.*

These pages show patterns made up of repeated small units. Like rolling out a patterned carpet, this type of pebblework makes an elegant and decorative feature in the landscape. It can be readily adapted to the external contours of buildings, and associates comfortably with other architectural elements.

The examples shown here are all on a large scale and not to be undertaken lightheartedly! The area of pebblework shown on page 25, chapter 2 is comparatively small, but it still took weeks of work.

The regularity of a repeated pattern is part of its fascination, so accurate setting-out is essential. Templates or stencils will often be used to define the shape and keep everything uniform. In Chinese patterns, a regular grid of stone or tile is set out first, and then the individual sections are filled in.

⏩ *A traditional Moorish pattern, Generalife Garden, Granada, Spain.*

Previous pages: (main photograph) Detail from Stevenson House mosaic before installation, Haddington, Scotland; (detail) Bas-relief fish mosaic in a churchyard, Archangelos, Rhodes.

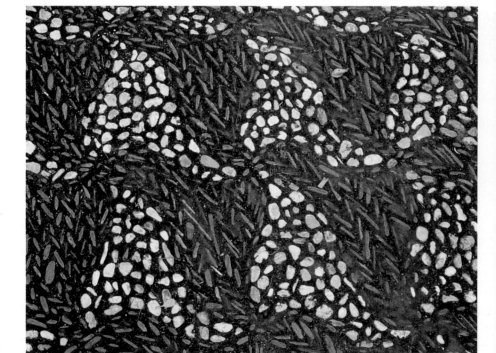

⬆ *A bold black and white scallopshell design. Funchal, Madeira.*

⬇ *A lovely crisp design by Matusan in traditional Turkish style. Antalya, Turkey.*

⬆ *Just one of the many repeat patterns invented by the Romans. This geometric design of squares and diagonals produces an optical 3-D effect. Conimbriga, Portugal.*

◀◀ *Another Moorish pattern based on overlapping circles. Cordoba, Spain.*

CHINESE ALLOVER PATTERNS

In the garden art of China, pebbles are used as the tiniest element in the overall composition of rock, water and plants. A pebble "carpet" is such an essential component that it is not surprising that there are so very many different patterns and their variations. The "bible" of Chinese landscape design, the *Yuan Yeh*, published in 1634, documents these patterns which are still being used today.

◖◗ *Interlocking crosses form a swastika pattern. Lines formed with gray granite strips are filled with a single color of pebble, which gives a contemporary feel to this newly created garden. Jichang Garden, Wuxi.*

The asymmetrical pattern known as "cracked ice." Xu Yuan, Nanjing.

A lovely pattern formed with sections of curved roof tile, filled with roughly broken limestone and tile shards.

Hexagons and diamonds are neatly tailored between the rock borders around a lake. Zhou Zheng Yuan, Suzhou.

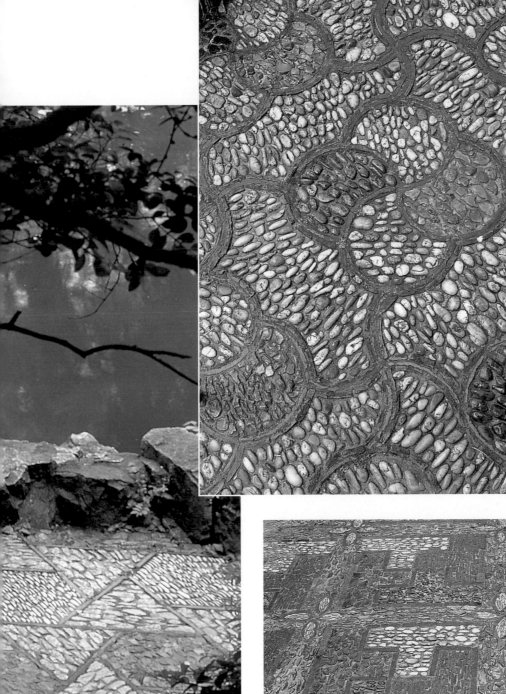

◀◀ *Another pattern formed with sections of roof tile filled with warm sandy-colored pebbles, black basalt pebbles and brilliant blue chunks of glass. Note how the outer portions of the pattern are emphasized with an additional strip of red tile, and how the pebbles are arranged diagonally from each "knot." Liu Yuan, Suzhou.*

◀ *A grid pattern that uses interlocking swastika squares with flowers at the intersections. There are six types of pebble within the stone-and-tile grid. Shizilin, Suzhou.*

INTERLACING PATTERNS

The invention of "knotwork" and interlacing designs is usually credited to the Celts, but this type of pattern appeared long before, in both Hittite and Egyptian cultures. As a separate development, Arab interlacing achieved great heights of geometric sophistication. It's an endlessly fascinating source of design ideas but, unfortunately, is often far too complex to be achieved in pebblework. Look instead for the smaller "knots" and patterns that are used in many crafts: stone carving, embroidery, metalwork, tiles, illuminated manuscripts and so on.

▶ *Celtic interlacing on a large scale in the Praça dos Restauradores. The crisply delineated knotwork in Portuguese mosaic technique adds a decorative grandeur to this city square. Lisbon, Portugal.*

▲ *Knotwork panels decorate this pebble mosaic path to a large townhouse. Funchal, Madeira.*

▶ *A design based on an interlaced "cross" motif.*

A design derived from a Moorish interlacing pattern and adapted for a pebble mosaic 13 ft (4 m) in diameter.

An interlacing design from Matusan.

A pebble mosaic based on a sampler stitched by Queen Elizabeth I. Interlacing patterns cross the boundaries of many art forms, and provide the source of many satisfying designs.

A design for an English "knot" garden.

ALLOVER CENTRICAL DESIGNS (REPEATING PATTERNS AROUND A CENTER)

These patterns start from a center point and radiate repeat elements regularly towards the perimeter. A different motif may be used to enhance the center, and enclosing borders are often used to round off the design. As this pattern is an underlying design element of carpets and ceramics, these are a happy hunting ground for pebble mosaic ideas.

 *Bold designs by the Turkish pebble mosaic company, Matusan.*
Top: Geometric "Seljuk" design.
Top right: An Ottoman design.
Above: A typical Turkish floral design.

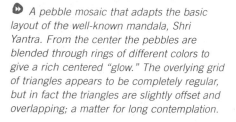 *A pebble mosaic that adapts the basic layout of the well-known mandala, Shri Yantra. From the center the pebbles are blended through rings of different colors to give a rich centered "glow." The overlying grid of triangles appears to be completely regular, but in fact the triangles are slightly offset and overlapping; a matter for long contemplation.*

202

🔄 *Concentric stars in bold black and white give a dynamic modern effect to this town plaza. Badajoz, Spain.*

🔄 *A design made with concentric circles and arcs producing a dramatic optical effect. The Romans, the Spanish and the Greeks have all used this design in various ways.*

BORDERS

A border will enhance even the smallest mosaic, giving it a frame and a feeling of completeness. Space permitting, more elaborate patterns are very rewarding, giving a "finish" to larger mosaics which is rich and carpet-like. They can also be used alone: wide borders look great around a garden feature, edging a plain area of paving, or running either side of a path.

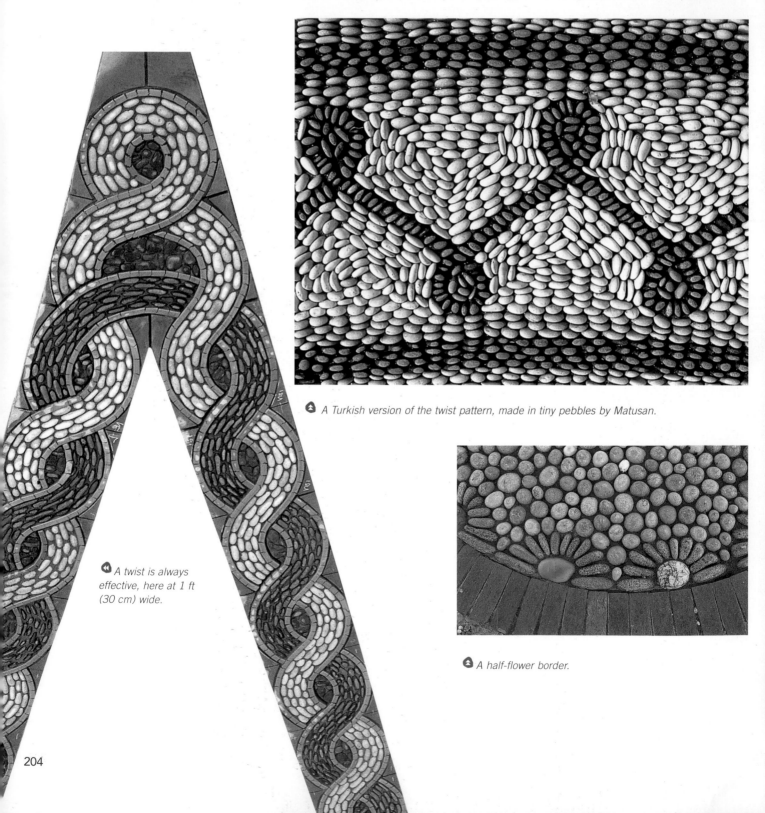

⬆ A Turkish version of the twist pattern, made in tiny pebbles by Matusan.

◀◀ A twist is always effective, here at 1 ft (30 cm) wide.

⬆ A half-flower border.

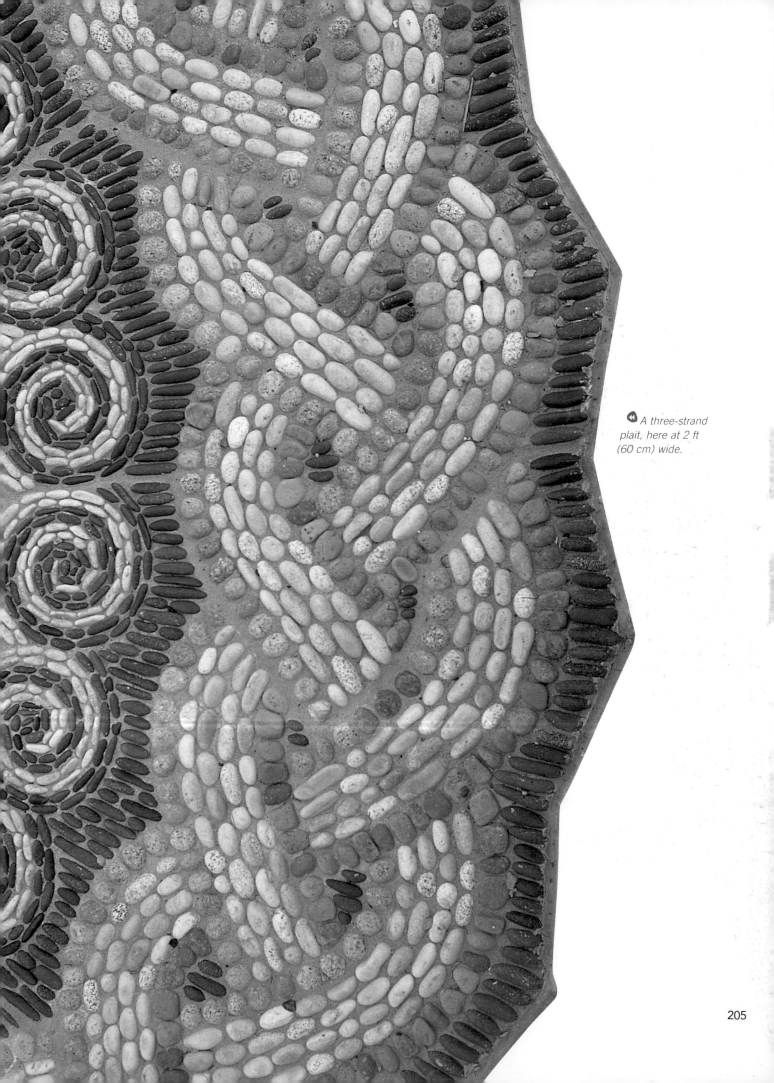

◀◀ *A three-strand plait, here at 2 ft (60 cm) wide.*

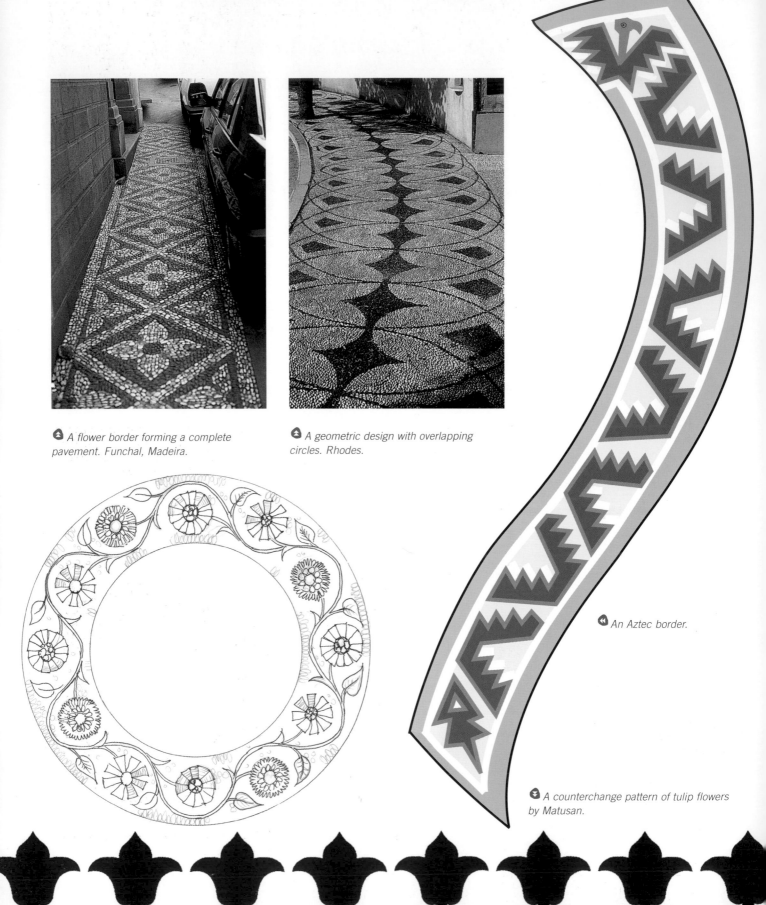

⬆ A flower border forming a complete pavement. Funchal, Madeira.

⬆ A geometric design with overlapping circles. Rhodes.

◀◀ An Aztec border.

⬇ A counterchange pattern of tulip flowers by Matusan.

The wave pattern, beloved by Greek and Romans and many others since. This version is at Pella, Greece (400 B.C.).

A classical scroll. This version is made of slate, with two carved pineapple finials. The two panels are designed to lie either side of a path and are 1 ft (30 cm) wide.

The wreath: another Roman pattern for a large-scale border.

⬆ *The very simplest of borders for small mosaics: long stones pointing inwards.*

⏩ *A modern design for a pavement border. Porto, Portugal.*

⏩ *From top to bottom:*
Interlocking diamonds make a good border.
A version of the plait, much used in Roman mosaics. In pebbles, it would need to be fairly wide, at least 20 in (50 cm).
A traditional North American pattern.

⬆ *Traditional Turkish "tulip" pattern, by Matusan.*

STARS

Stars are timeless universal emblems that can vary from the simplest motif to complex and decorated pictures. Always easy to recognize, pleasing and uncontroversial, they can be either formal and sharp or loose and more expressive.

▶▶ A star by Matusan in tiny black and white pebbles. A flower makes a pleasing contrast in the center. Antalya, Turkey.

⬇ A four-pointed star, also known as St. John's Cross. Arkholme Church, U.K..

⬇ A five-pointed star with Moorish interlacing. Design for a mosaic 6 ft 6 in (2 m) in diameter.

△ *Visually, the compass is closely related to the star and makes an effective subject for pebble mosaic. Here it forms the floor of a garden gazebo and incorporates letters for its four cardinal points. Slate makes an interesting flat contrasting surface on the compass points.*

▷ *A 12 pointed version in many colors which I call "Exploding Star." The design was generated entirely on the computer. Design for a mosaic 8 ft (2.5 m) in diameter.*

SUN AND MOON

⬆ *The rays of the sun dominate this swirling design. Traditional Greek black and white pebblework at Archangelos, Rhodes.*

⏩ *A more complex version of the sun motif that is almost a Catherine wheel. It is surrounded by a wavy border representing water. Stockton-on-Tees, U.K.*

⬇ *A Turkish design by Matusan, which they call "Charcofelek," portrays both the sun and a spinning wheel. Antalya, Turkey.*

A simple sun with wavy rays is always a popular motif. The colors have been selected to grade through red, brown-yellow, pale yellow to bright white, and are contrasted against a background of black pebbles flowing in the opposite direction: 4 ft 8 in (1.5 m) in diameter.

The moon is a good motif for a simple mosaic. But this one's not so simple. I've waxed lyrical, borrowing an idea from Mexico of a sleeping feminine moon which rests in a scallop shell. The mosaic forms the base of a shallow pool and the moon appears to be a reflection from above. East Cleveland Hospital, U.K.

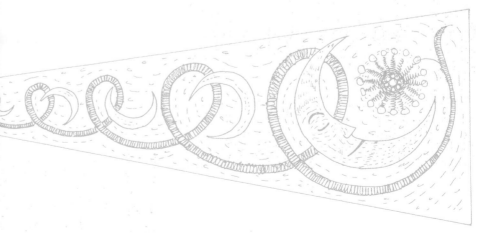

⬆ *I love the simplicity of this pebble mosaic spiral by Ula Siegers. Slender, earth-colored stones are graded to length and carefully placed in the spiral form of a fossil ammonite. Private garden, Germany.*

⬇ *This design is made for a mosaic 16 ft (5 m) in diameter. Like a cornucopia of good things, waves and fishes disgorge from the spiraling shell. This mosaic was designed to be made in graded colors for a 3-D effect in a seaside location.*

A seaside venue and a Christian view of the millennium celebrations led to this maze design. The labyrinth represents a spiritual journey within the physical form of a fish, an early Christian symbol.

An interesting subject for mosaics, the maze takes many forms. This one was adapted from the large maze at Ely Cathedral, U.K. There are lots of books available for information and, once you've got the hang of it, you'll find no difficulty in designing your own. Whitehaven, U.K.

The Miners' Memorial mosaic. The cross is in black granite, representing the coal, which is overlaid by a wheel, symbol of the pit-head winding-gear. The mosaic commemorates the terrible loss of life throughout the working history of the local mines. Its border incorporates images of the sea, fire and explosions. Whitehaven, U.K.

The Chinese yin-yang symbol of perfect balance between opposites: two black and white shapes combine to form a circle. Pebble mosaic in the Guqi Garden, Shanghai, China.

HUMAN FIGURES

There's nothing quite as tricky as representing *us*, the human species. Let's face it, we're never quite comfortable with the way we look. What should be done about clothes, how do you make believable eyes and should you try for a three-dimensional effect? When we think of the human form we always think about beauty, and whether we are representing a person properly. We project our own hang-ups onto the image.

A QUESTION OF REALISM

A big problem is our desire for visual realism. At the very beginning of pebble mosaic history, the ancient Greeks were fascinated by realism. For instance, take a look at "The Deer Hunt" with its detailed realistic musculature and three-dimensionality. We can imagine the pebble artist (he spread his name, "Gnosis," over the background) carefully drawing the whole picture and then shading particular areas from light through to dark, and meticulously organizing the execution of the picture. The pebbles are graded into several tones and used to achieve a beautiful rounding of the body form.

So what's the problem? The muscular realism and three-dimensionality are amazing. But look again. The picture is so perfectly worked out that the figures look frozen, rooted to the spot. The attempts to suggest movement by making the cloaks whirl out and hats fly off look rather wooden. There's something about the figure of the stag that makes it look as though it's made of plastic, almost like a Bambi cartoon.

I don't want to underestimate Gnosis' fantastic achievement, but I do think that there are some interesting lessons to be learned from his attempts to create realism using nothing more than pebbles. They can only do so much. No matter how carefully they are selected and graded, they are, after all, only blobs of colored stone.

These colored blobs are the raw material that we are working with. Each pebble we place becomes a single mark in the mosaic, in much the same way as a brush loaded with color makes its mark on a painting. Our eyes and brains assemble all these pieces of information, marks of paint or pebble, into a coherent image. For me, this is exactly where the excitement and mystery of pebblework lies: in the way that ordinary pebbles are used to suggest something quite different. The pebbles are all we have to make the picture, so we must find exactly the right pebble for the effect we want to make in our drawing of the human figure. My motto has always been: "Let the stones speak."

The stones are the key to success. Let's forget realism. That way we gain the freedom to explore anything, no matter how fantastic; to make legendary, mythical, anthropomorphic creatures, gods and heroes, symbolic creatures, simplified emblems of youth and old age. Of course, we still have to be rigorous in our drawing, but now we're free to let the pebbles create rhythms and textures, and to work with the natural organic properties of the medium.

◢ Using a rich mixture of colors selected from Mexican beach pebbles, the artist, Christine Desmond, has achieved an evocative portrait. A truly pointillist technique: half-shut your eyes and see how the three stones for each white of the eyes merge into one. The stylized hair pattern and the herringbone fronds of the greenery and necklace make use of the attractive patterns so easily achieved in pebblework.

◄◄ "The Deer Hunt," a pebble mosaic in the palace of Alexander the Great (c. 4 B.C.), Pella, northern Greece. Larger than life-size figures are modeled in several shades—highlights, mid-tones, darks—with lines of small black pebbles to outline the figures and increase definition. The stag has two additional tones of ginger coloring on its body, and spots. It demonstrates a highly disciplined process: Gnosis, the pebble artist, interpreting a meticulously designed and painted cartoon. It's interesting to see how the pebbles, though tiny, are uniform in size and are first arranged in rows to follow the outlines and main muscle shadows, and thereafter filled in to follow the shading plan.

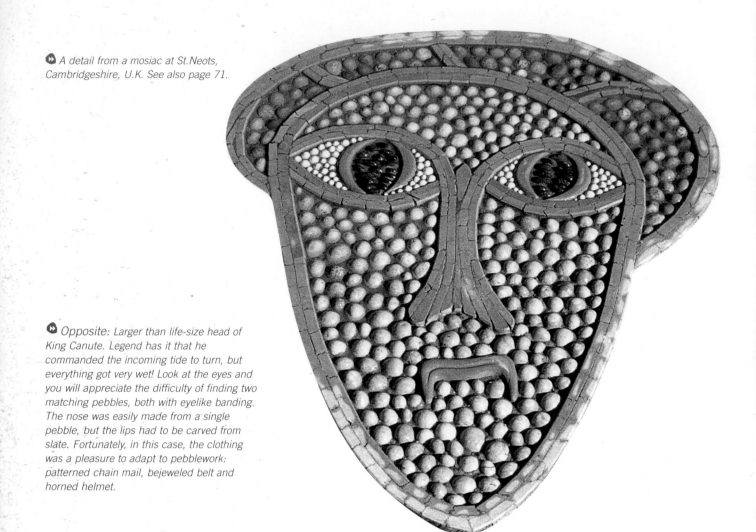

A detail from a mosaic at St.Neots, Cambridgeshire, U.K. See also page 71.

Opposite: Larger than life-size head of King Canute. Legend has it that he commanded the incoming tide to turn, but everything got very wet! Look at the eyes and you will appreciate the difficulty of finding two matching pebbles, both with eyelike banding. The nose was easily made from a single pebble, but the lips had to be carved from slate. Fortunately, in this case, the clothing was a pleasure to adapt to pebblework: patterned chain mail, bejeweled belt and horned helmet.

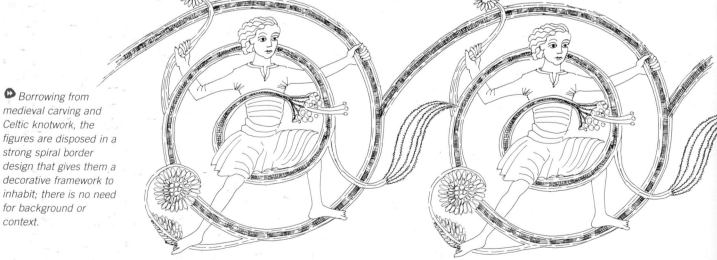

Borrowing from medieval carving and Celtic knotwork, the figures are disposed in a strong spiral border design that gives them a decorative framework to inhabit; there is no need for background or context.

ON CLOTHING AND STYLE

I have always found that clothes are a problem in pebblework. Instead of concentrating on expressing the shape of the body and the power of its movement, you find yourself fussing about how to do a collar or shoes in pebbles. I'd sooner not! Hair is easy flowing stuff, but hats are a pain. And then there are those sudden exposed bits of flesh needing a different treatment: a color, shading, more realism. The only time I tried to design figures with historical accuracy, I found that the result was the most boring mosaic I have ever made. You won't see a picture of it in this book— although, I regret to say, the mosaic still exists.

Stylized figures, however, appear to lie naturally on the groundscape that's made by pebble mosaics. The conflict that exists between a naturalistic image and its flattened pebble rendition disappears. We accept the unreality of the figures instantly, and immediately begin to appreciate the underlying agenda of the stylization. Do the figures luxuriate in an eternal outflowing cornucopia of good things? Are they spinning in a heavenly sphere?

The inspiration of Greek vase-painting underlies these black and white figures in this design for a large pavement in the Eden Project, Cornwall. Somehow the black figures appear warm and their nakedness quite natural, and the style of the white sgraffito lines emphasizes the muscles within the silhouettes.

Black pebbles and a stylized design overcome the problem of "Virgo" (astrological sign for the dates August 23–September 23). She is a mythical figure of fruitfulness and fertility. Sometimes represented as a golden-haired angel, she is here clothed as an Egyptian goddess, jewels irradiating her wings.

"Childhood" and "Age," two drawings for mosaics on the theme of the Seven Ages of Man. Again, black and white makes for direct expression.

MYTHOLOGICAL FIGURES AND ANTHROPOMORPHIC CREATURES

These subjects, semihuman in form, inhabit an imaginary world: mermaid, Neptune, centaur, sphinx, angels and cupids, satyrs, witches, the Devil; and a thousand more. Their charm is that they can fly in the heavens, live comfortably under the sea, associate naturally with dangerous animals and creatures of all types, and thus lend themselves to dramas and stories which endlessly fascinate. They are superreal. They have no problems with the day-to-day reality of things: right way up, upside down, background or space, three-dimensionality, skin color or clothing. No wonder they are always popular subjects that lift us from the mundane to a dreamworld where anything can happen.

Mermaid and Neptune from my large mosaic in Bournemouth. The mermaid lazes in her shell bed extending a webbed hand to Neptune who, in a kingly pose, holds a sea horse and starfish torch, like an orb and scepter. He has seashells in his hair, and an octopus headdress. The mermaid sports her traditional scaly fish tail, while Neptune enjoys a double interwoven version. Showing naked breasts in public places is no problem when they're rendered in pebbles. They are a part of a mythic creature and not at all sensuous.

⬆ *Stick figures made from riven shards of black slate. When slate is split along the grain, the character of the irregular and spiky pieces can be exploited to express parts of a figure—a useful technique, especially when space is limited. These figures are less than a foot (30 cm) high.*

⬇ *A slate stick figure against a background of pea gravel. This small mosaic was a prototype for a school project. Size: 15 in x 18 in (37.5 cm x 45 cm).*

STICK FIGURES

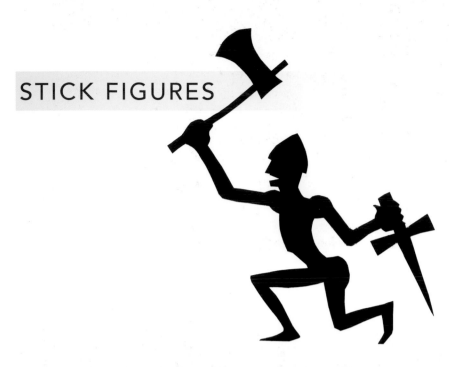

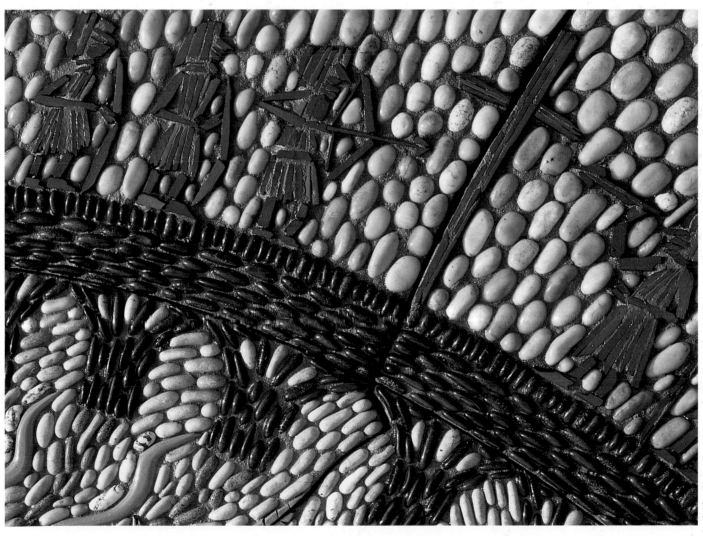

Tiny slate stick figures, only 8 in (20 cm) high, represent soldiers preparing for a fight on Stirling Bridge.

ANIMALS

Images of animals made in pebble mosaic can vary from realistically observed portraits to highly stylized decorative designs. Whatever the style, the same rules apply: aim for clarity, with a good contrast between the animal and its background. A recognizable silhouette and characteristic pose are usually best. Head-on views are generally pretty difficult to sort out (one set of legs behind another, and all behind the head!). Rear and overhead views are much the same. The side view is most often used, and can show the typical

movements of the animal: running or springing, or baring its teeth.

Animals vary in size from enormous to tiny, so their scale needs some consideration. The larger the animal the more it will need to be shrunk, and vice versa for the smallest. They need to be large enough to be able to take some detailing. For instance, animals like a hedgehog or mouse may seem to be easy subjects, but can end up appearing as little more than a blob. A good characteristic outline is required with a few carefully chosen and executed details. The animal's eye is important and needs to be precisely positioned, or the whole thing looks wrong.

A fierce bull. Plenty of liberties have been taken to emphasize his strength and bad temper. This drawing has been made on the computer from an initial sketch. It indicates the shading that will be used, and the direction in which the pebbles are to be laid.

There's not a lot of "shape" to a sheep, so the design concentrates attention on the dainty carved feet and horns. The texture of the round white limestone pebbles suggests the wool, contrasting well with the background of black "longs" radiating from the center. Butcher's shop, Hornby, U.K.

⬆ *The design of this Chinese dragon was derived from illustrations of antique Chinese lacquer and metalware. Adapting the basic idea to pebblework called for some simplification: clarifying and rearranging the whiskers and flames. Angular red stones on the body suggest scales, and the background cloud-scrolls help to fix the oriental style.*

⬆ ⬅ *A squirrel and stag in a pebble mosaic developed from the drawings below.*
• *A mixture of brown flints and red granite pebbles were used to approximate to the rich brown colors of these animals.*
• *To increase the 3-D effect, thin rows were used at the edges with fatter rows in the center of the bodies.*
• *Darker pebbles were used on the legs of the stag and around the jawline.*
• *Pebble lines flow with the forms of the limbs and muscles.*
• *Because the color tone of the animals is not greatly different from the background color, the textural contrast helps definition: long pebbles for the animals, round ones for the background.*
SQUIRREL BY MARK CURRIE, STAG BY JANETTE IRELAND; BOTH TO MY DESIGN FOR THE STEVENSON HOUSE MOSAIC, HADDINGTON, SCOTLAND.

➲ A head alone, heraldic in style, surrounded by a sun-ray border. This is a small mosaic 4 ft (1.2 m) in diameter. Size often dictates the form that the subject must take. At this scale, a lion complete with body would have to be so simplified as to make it quite characterless; whereas the head alone allows scope for interesting teeth and flowing sunlike mane. It represents the astrological sign of Leo. Gresgarth Hall garden, U.K.

➲ The leopard's body is made with yellow quartz; the spots are a darker yellow with black surrounds. A real leopard has many more spots, but it was impossible to get any more in at this size. The leopard is the symbol of the county of Shropshire and is placed against a background map. Shrewsbury, U.K..

➲ Drawing of a leopard, adjusted to fit into an oval-shaped design.

Eyes are so important! However carefully the rest of the pebblework is made, one false move with the eye can spoil the effect. This is what has happened here in this sign of Capricorn, a goat with a fish tail. Some of the scales from the tail have been "borrowed" to make a pretty border round the goat's head. Gresgarth Hall garden, U.K.

An expressive dragon's head in Chinese style. The artist has focused on the alarming teeth and staring eyes to make this a terrifying creature. The head is delineated with tile and white ceramic shards. Guqi Garden, Shanghai, China.

REPTILES AND FISH

These are good subjects for the garden. They are particularly suitable for pools and fountains, where warm-blooded creatures can sometimes appear rather odd—possibly drowned. Characteristic outlines, fins and magical colors all help to make good designs.

⊘ *The drawing here is very stylized (the back legs no more than a mark), but it is clearly a frog. Using the typical Chinese method, the outlines are made in sections of black roof tile which are filled with a pattern of black pebbles, white ceramic shards and blue glass. Zhou Zheng Yuan, Shanghai, China.*

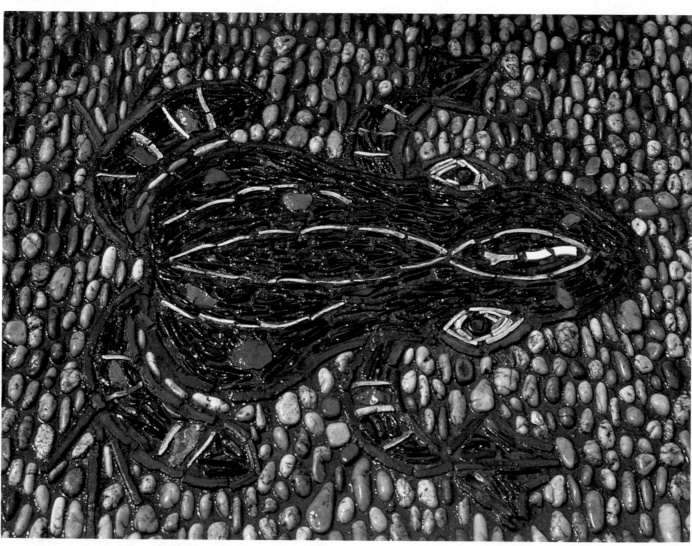

◀ Is this a fish, or is it half fish, half seahorse? Playful and amusing, it decorates a spa at Eva Piges, Rhodes.

◀ Nearly all lizards have interesting shapes. Mark Davidson has added a Polynesian patterning to his gecko mosaic so that it stands out dramatically against the black background.

▶ Fanciful fish! Nevertheless, they have some characteristics of real fish. Carved slate tails and fins are a helpful detail; the white underbellies and fish-scale patterns add to their credibility. Glass nuggets enhance the fishy look of the scales.

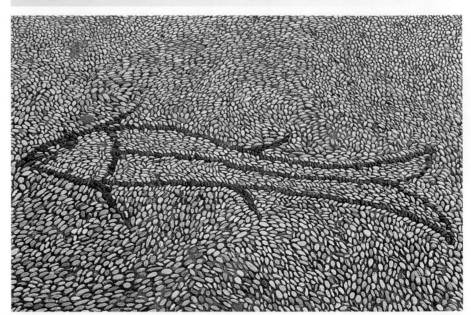

⏩ *Fish mosaic in a churchyard. A simple outline drawing in black and white: elegant, well observed and carefully detailed. Archangelos, Rhodes.*

⏬ *The many tentacles of the octopus give a lot of scope for filling the space with decorative swirls. The "suckers" are made from single white pebbles, and the "eyes" are exaggerated like a cartoon, so that the octopus becomes comic rather than frightening. A fountain in Bradford, U.K.*

234

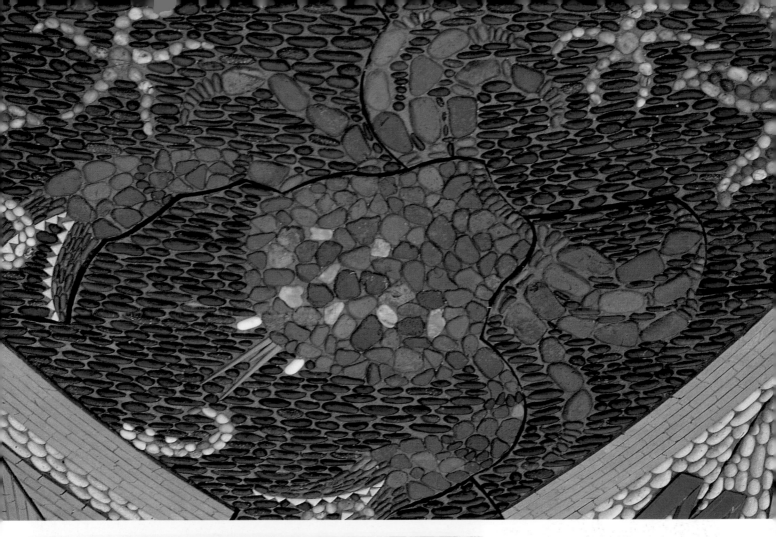

⬆ Angular red granite stones suggest the carapace of this crab. The legs were difficult because there are so many of them. Each one comprises several segments, which were made from selected large stones. Bradford, U.K..

◀◀ A lovely fish by Joel Baker of Naturescape. With the characteristic fish outline clearly established, the decorative possibilities of a range of colors and attractive patterns are exploited to the full. Burton Agnes Hall garden, U.K.

BIRDS

⬆ *It's hard to do birds on a small scale. This swallow is about a foot (30 cm) long. Using only a few pebbles and shards of slate, it expresses the color and movement of a swallow in flight. BY PRU GLOSSOP, AT MELLING, U.K.*

⬆ *A heron, with its characteristic shape, makes a good subject. In this mosaic it is approximately life-size, giving space for plenty of detail in the feathering, a simple border and some background decoration.*

⬆ *Two cranes: much-loved birds in China. Modern pebblework made in black tile and white ceramic shards against a sandy-colored background. Chou Cheng Yuan, Suzhou, China.*

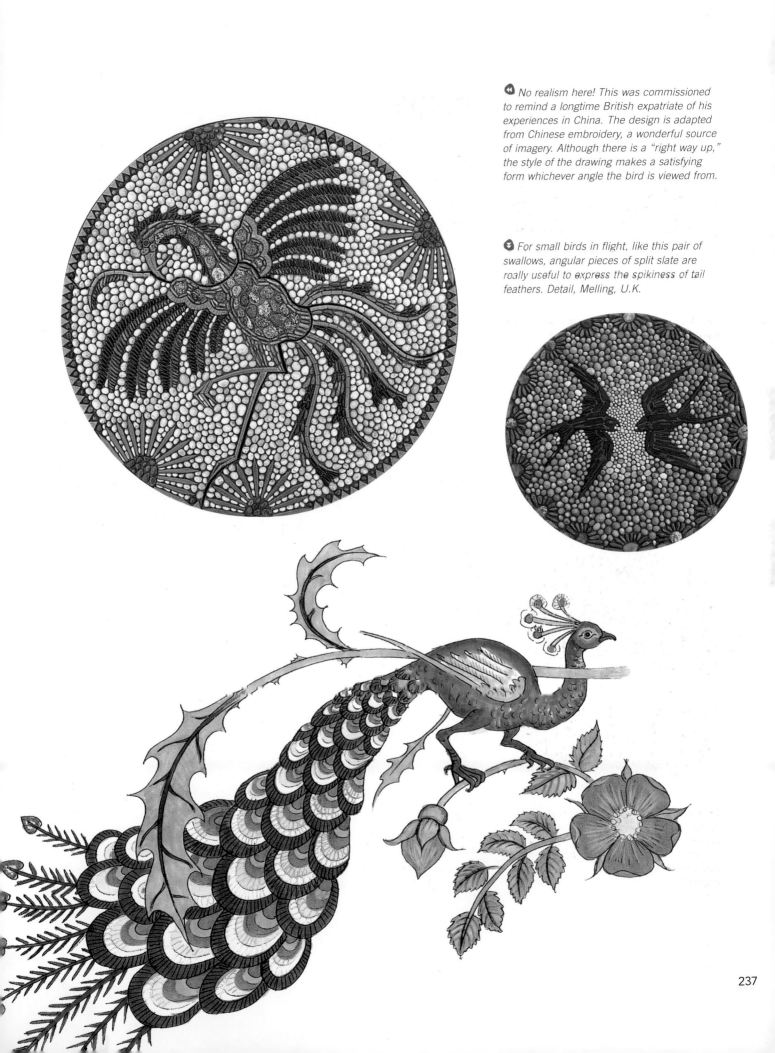

◀◀ *No realism here! This was commissioned to remind a longtime British expatriate of his experiences in China. The design is adapted from Chinese embroidery, a wonderful source of imagery. Although there is a "right way up," the style of the drawing makes a satisfying form whichever angle the bird is viewed from.*

⊗ *For small birds in flight, like this pair of swallows, angular pieces of split slate are really useful to express the spikiness of tail feathers. Detail, Melling, U.K.*

237

It's great fun playing with colored pebbles, trying to catch the markings of the feathers. Some ingenuity and a lot of artistic license make this owl a jolly bird. The National Portrait Gallery, Edinburgh, Scotland.

A perching pheasant. The carved details of beak and feet add credibility. The colors on the head are amazonite and red jasper: appropriately bright like the pheasant's exotic plumage. Detail, Lytham, U.K.

This owes more to fantasy than realistic observation. Decorative qualities have been exploited in the bird's claws, tail and feathers. Everything was adapted to fit neatly into a roundel. Whipps Cross Hospital, London, U.K.

A graceful subject. The swan's plumage display is expressed by bands of pebbles of selected sizes. Finding just the right pebble for the beak and nasal-mound was quite a challenge: 3 ft 4 in (1 m) in diameter. BY ALI WOOD TO MY DESIGN.

239

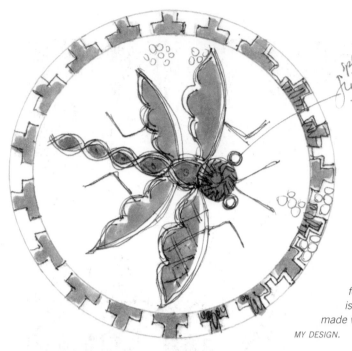

split flint eyes

INSECTS

◀◀ *Design for a stylized Chinese dragonfly. To be outlined with slate strips or ceramic shards; the wings to be filled with blue glass nuggets: 4 ft (1.2 m) in diameter.*

◥ *Sometimes it's enjoyable to try to achieve a very realistic effect. Allowing for some artistic latitude, and many compromises with the pebbles, this mosaic is modeled on the European peacock butterfly. Both feelers and body are made with black ceramic shards. Detail, Lytham, U.K. MADE BY RUSSELL SMALLWOOD TO MY DESIGN.*

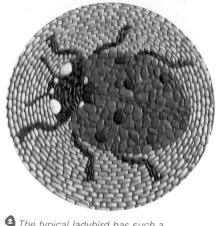

The typical ladybird has such a characteristic shape and color that it's easy to recognize. However, it's difficult to get the legs thin enough, and hard to find stones that are red enough.

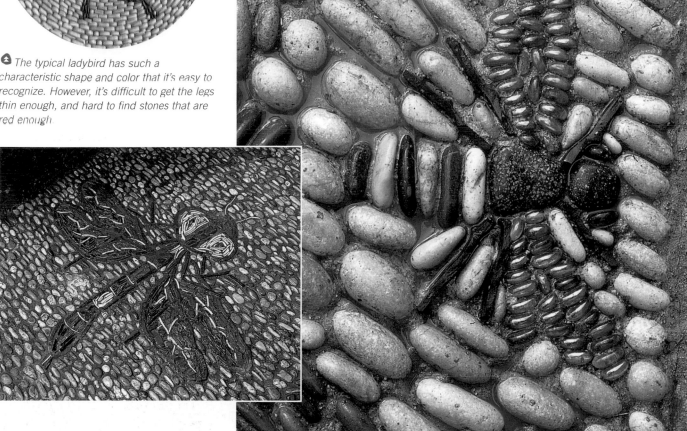

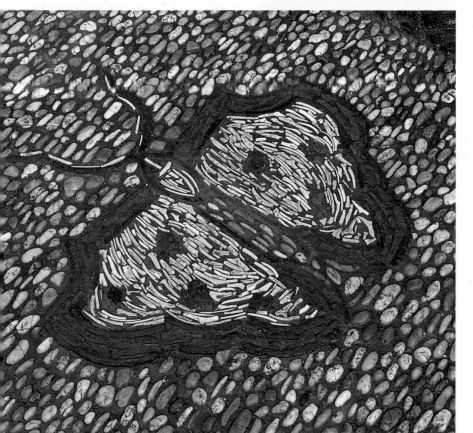

A little honeybee made of eight pebbles, a few pieces of black china and glass nuggets for wings. Extremely simple, and yet it still measures 8 in (20 cm) in length. BY JOHN TALLON; IN THE MELLING MOSAIC, U.K.

I'm not familiar enough with Chinese entomology to know whether this insect is real or imaginary, but it matters little. The interesting details of wing pattern, eyes, feelers and stinger are entertainment enough. Zhou Zheng Yuan, Suzhou, China.

Chinese mosaicists rely heavily on the use of ceramic shards. They give a fine detailed texture to the wings of this butterfly. The body of the insect is outlined with black roof tile sections, which are then filled in (another much-used technique). It's a logical way to work: first make the drawing, and then fill in with decoration afterwards. Zhou Zheng Yuan, Suzhou, China.

FLOWERS

A flower can be one of the simplest of motifs; but on the other hand, all the different species and their botanical intricacies can be exploited in a thousand different ways. Many flowers are endowed with a particular symbolism in different cultures. Some are borrowed by clubs and campaigns. They can have an entirely personal meaning too, for an individual or a specific location.

A mosaic path of flowers swirling around a hospital courtyard. Some of the flowers are moderately realistic, some entirely imaginary. They are linked together by the twisting pattern of their stems and leaves. Whipps Cross Hospital, London, U.K.

Another recurring theme for mosaic: flowers in a pot. For clarity, there should not be too many flowers, and they should have an interesting shape. Here, the blooms are oriental and the pot decorated. Zhou Zheng Yuan, Suzhou, China.

The central motif of this design is an aster-like flower. Note how the design has the actual pebbles drawn onto it. The drawing is at 1:10 scale, and when blown up to actual size, will be 5 ft x 2 ft 7 in (approximately 1.5 m x 80 cm).

◀◀ *A brand new mosaic in a village square. This simple eight-petaled flower makes a bold splash in the resurfaced road. The landscapers have used colors and stone types that are found throughout the village. It's good that these traditional features have been reinstated, while the rest of the surface has been updated with durable granite setts. Cerro, Italy.*

⬆ *A simple and effective flower design by Matusan.*

⏪ *Lovely simple flowers made by Pete Flowers in the Melling mosaic. Inspiration came from a collection of ceramic "rings" which are in fact the broken-off necks of old beer flagons which had been thrown into the local river. These form the centers of the flowers from which the pebble petals radiate in rings of color.*

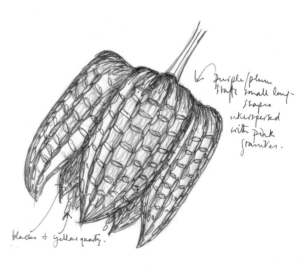

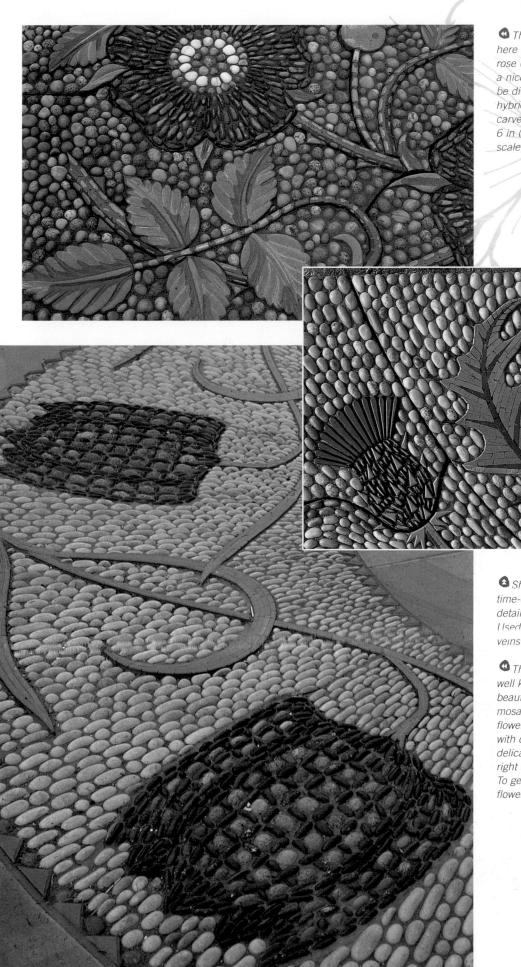

◄◄ That potent symbol, the rose, is shown here in the single-petaled form of the wild rose (also beloved of heraldic devices). It has a nice clear shape and pattern. Clarity would be difficult in a rose of many petals like the hybrid tea. The rose leaves here have been carved in bas-relief on slate approximately 6 in (15 cm) long, because pebbles, on this scale, would have yielded insufficient detail.

◓ Shaping and carving pieces of slate is time-consuming, but enables you to achieve details that are difficult with pebbles alone. Used to good effect here in the prickles and veins of this thistle at Stirling, U.K.

◄◄ The village where this mosaic is situated is well known as a habitat for a particularly beautiful wild plant, the fritillary, so this mosaic had to be about fritillaries. Their flowers are a very particular pinkish purple with dark reticulation, and their leaves form delicate straplike strands. Getting just the right shape and color of stones was difficult. To get the correct detail, the size of the flowers had to be 1 ft 8 in (50 cm) square.

245

TREES

Trees remind us of growth, strength and nature. Their branches are home to birds, animals and insects. They can also support and entwine many other expressive symbols. Only their size presents us with a problem. Either the mosaic must be very large or, if not, then the design has to be very much simplified.

⬆ *A large "Tree of Life" can be seen at Burton Agnes Hall, Yorkshire, U.K. A decorative tree with scroll-like branches, it measures 33 ft (10 m) in length. This size is appropriate to the scale of the surrounding landscape garden and can accommodate a good deal of detail. But be warned! Pebble mosaic on this scale is a very considerable undertaking, demanding months of planning and hard work in its execution.* BY NATURESCAPE TO AN ORIGINAL DESIGN BY CATHERINE LUCAS.

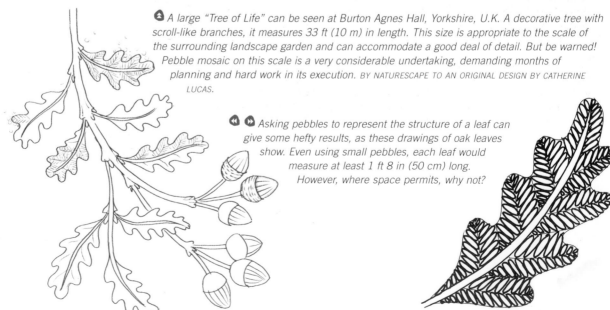

◀ ▶ *Asking pebbles to represent the structure of a leaf can give some hefty results, as these drawings of oak leaves show. Even using small pebbles, each leaf would measure at least 1 ft 8 in (50 cm) long. However, where space permits, why not?*

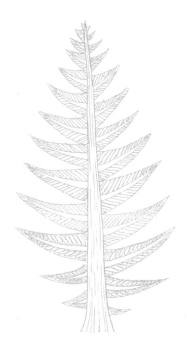

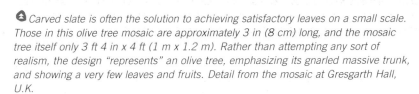 *Carved slate is often the solution to achieving satisfactory leaves on a small scale. Those in this olive tree mosaic are approximately 3 in (8 cm) long, and the mosaic tree itself only 3 ft 4 in x 4 ft (1 m x 1.2 m). Rather than attempting any sort of realism, the design "represents" an olive tree, emphasizing its gnarled massive trunk, and showing a very few leaves and fruits. Detail from the mosaic at Gresgarth Hall, U.K.*

Attempts to scale down the tree motif for small mosaics produced these designs for pine and fir trees. The different characteristic branching of each tree has been both simplified and emphasized to produce an interesting silhouette. The pine tree will have bunches of "needles" shaped in slate, and carved cones. The fir tree has a spiky outline and would be made from slate strips and pebbles.

OTHER SUITABLE SUBJECTS FOR PEBBLE MOSAIC

I have always found all natural organic subjects to be a rich source of ideas for pebble mosaic themes. Far less satisfying are those connected with straight lines, mathematical precision and machines. I find their attributes contradict the essentially random, variable and suggestive qualities of pebbles. So why use a medium so unsympathetic and unsuitable? Far better to engrave those designs onto steel or glass, or sandblast onto polished stone. Using these materials and techniques will achieve impressive detail, razor-edged execution and an "untouched" look. So, for pebble mosaic, all forms of mechanical devices make poor subjects, as do maps and diagrams. Architecture can be attempted, but only if the buildings have characteristic details that can be simplified and exaggerated.

◀◀ *A simple castle based on an heraldic design. Square-shaped river-worn sandstones are to be used for the walls, suggesting the massive masonry of the ancient castle.*

⧨ *A fanciful castle in black and white; the design is derived from a medieval woodcut of Stirling (Strevelyn) Castle. It bears no resemblance whatsoever to the existing building, but makes an attractive design with exaggerated flags and towers and simplified battlements. Stirling Museum, Scotland U.K.*

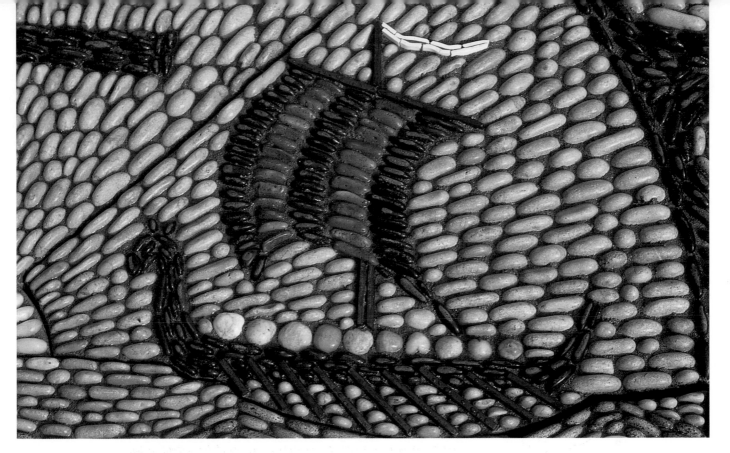

⬆ *Ships are good subjects. This small Roman ship is simplified a great deal, but it still has a recognizable figurehead, shields and oars. To be seen clearly, larger sailing ships would need to be shown in side view and the many sails should be separated.*

⬇ *A scallop shell. Slate strips add definition and establish the gradual curves of the shell. The basic drawing of a subject like this needs care; otherwise, it can easily look like a blob.*

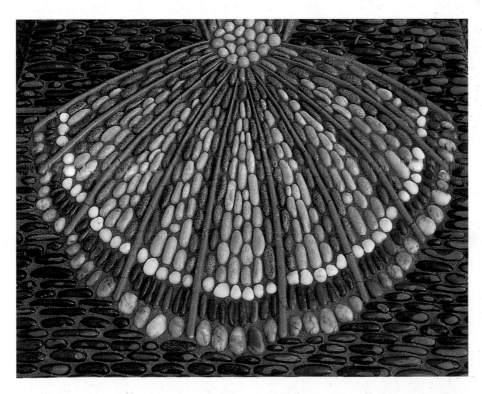

⬆ *A decorative urn from a Roman mosaic.*

TEACHING & LEARNING

All fired up and ready to go...

When artists discover the possibilities of pebble mosaics and begin to experiment with them, they encounter a steep learning curve. They find that the craft requires a wide range of knowledge in a number of disciplines: geology, concrete technology, stone-working and landscape design, in addition to all its artistic considerations. So it's not surprising that cries for help have flooded in to me from around the world, and in increasing volume. I had hoped that the sections, "Making a Pebble Mosaic" in my first book, and "Core Techniques" in the present volume would provide enough information for beginners to get started; and this has certainly proved true for a number of dedicated individuals, some of whom feature in this new edition. However, learning alone, like taking a correspondence course, is not for everyone, and the demand for teaching workshops grew to the point where it could no longer be ignored.

Since 2004 there have been four annual summer schools at Cobblestone Designs' workshop, and in 2007 new classes were held in the Chicago School of Mosaic, U.S. I find that when people make such an effort to travel long distances to attend my classes, it is a real pleasure to teach them. A great deal gets done in the short time available, and students are able to make enduring network contacts.

At the same time, it is important to acknowledge that there are other teachers running pebble mosaic workshops. They tend to concentrate on non-functional mosaics for walls and various decorative indoor uses, while my own strategy for teaching new pebble artists is to encourage and concentrate solely upon techniques that are permanent in all conditions. What I teach is definitely "art to be walked on," and is intended to last for a hundred years and more.

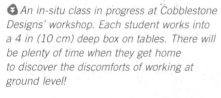

Students on a basic course at the Chicago School of Mosaic have made pebble mosaics-in-a-box, which are easier for workshop conditions than working on-the-knees. The results are all placed together for a discussion so that students learn from each others' successes and failures.

An in-situ class in progress at Cobblestone Designs' workshop. Each student works into a 4 in (10 cm) deep box on tables. There will be plenty of time when they get home to discover the discomforts of working at ground level!

The Chicago School of Mosaic hosted this pre-cast course in 2007. Every student made three small pieces to take home. The first two were exercises in pebble types and patterns; the ones shown here were made to the students' own designs. The School runs courses in all types of mosaic and regularly invites prominent mosaic artists from abroad to share their skills. (www.chicagomosaicschool.com)

One-to-one assistance; exploring the details of interpreting a design in pebbles.

A good result for Rob Tester in his third and final mosaic of the course. He shows an understanding of stone shape, color contrast and drawing, as well as mastering the tricky "upside-down" technique. It's a lot to pull together in four and a half days.

An exciting moment when the slab is turned over and the mosaic revealed for the first time! Sue Rew, brushing the sand from her double frond design.

Appendices

A. SELECTED FURTHER READING

BAIRRADA, EDUARDO M. *Empedrados Artisticos de Lisboa*. Lisbon, publisher unknown, 1985.
A complete survey, with some English translation, of Lisbon's mosaic pavements.

BALE, JEFFREY. "My Approach to Pebble Mosaic", article in *American Landscape Architecture* magazine No.8/2005. Also, in the same issue, an article about Jeffrey Bale, "Ancient Futures" by J.M. Cava.
_____. "Create a Pebble Mosaic", article in *Fine Gardening* magazine No. 82/2001.

BÜHLER, ERNST. *Natursteinmosaike*. Stuttgart, Verlag Paul Haupt, 2001.
The "stone art" of Swiss teacher Ernst Bühler and his pupils, including Johannes Vielmetter.

CHENG, JI. *The Craft of Gardens*. New Haven and London, Yale University Press, 1988.
A translation of the original manual "Yuan Yeh" of 1634.

DUNBABIN, CATHERINE. *Mosaics of the Greek and Roman World*. Cambridge, Cambridge University Press, 2001.
An authoritative scholarly survey.

HOWARTH, MAGGY. *The Art of Pebble Mosaic*. Tunbridge Wells, Search Press, 1994.
My first book, concentrating on basic principles, to which this book is a sequel.

KESWICK, MAGGIE. *The Chinese Garden*. London, Academy Editions, 1978, 1986. New York, St. Martins Press, 1986.
An invaluable introduction to Chinese garden art.

LOUKIANOS, YIANNIS. *The Pebbled Yards of the Aegean*. Athens, publisher unknown, 1998.
_____. *The Pebbly Yards of Cyclades*. Athens, publisher unknown, 1998.
Insight into the style and techniques of Greek pebble mosaics.

LING, ROGER. *Ancient Mosaics*. London, British Museum Press, 1998.

MASSON, GEORGINA. *Italian Gardens*. London, Thames & Hudson, 1961.
Still the best guide to Italian Renaissance gardens.

WILLIM, MARIANNE AND R. BUHL. *Pflastermosaiken in Freiburg*. Freiburg, Promo Verlag GmbH, 2000.
About the traditional designs of Freiburg, with split-pebble technique.

B. DIRECTORY OF PEBBLE MOSAIC ARTISTS

Note: Some of the artists featured in this book prefer to retain their privacy. This list, therefore, only contains those who would welcome enquiries for mosaic commissions or other work as described under each entry. In alphabetical order:

ALDO, DEB
Cincinatti, U.S.
Web: www.pietreduredesign.com
email: deb@pietreduredesign.com
Pebble mosaics and garden design

ANDERSEN, GLEN
Vancouver, Canada
Web: www.mosaicplanet@mac.com
email: mosaicplanet@mac.com
Pebble mosaics and community projects

BAKER, JOEL
Edinburgh, U.K.
email: joelbakermosaics@googlemail.com
Pebble mosaic and garden design

BALE, JEFFERY
Oregon, U.S.
Web: www.jeffreygardens.com
email: jeffreygardens@earthlink.net
Pebble mosaics and gardens

BOTICA, JOHN
Auckland, New Zealand
Web: www.powerofpebbles.com
email: john@powerofpebbles.com
Pebble mosaics

CARMAN, KEVIN
Florida, U.S.
Web: www.kcmosaic.biz
email: lamicus1@yahoo.com
Pebble and tile mosaics

CHIOSTRINI, FABRIZIO
Florence, Italy
email: fabriziochiostrini@hotmail.com
Pebble mosaic and garden fantasies

CLARKE, WENDY
Dirtscape Dreaming, Victoria, Australia
Web: www.dirtscapedreaming.com.au
email: info@dirtscapedreaming.com.au
Landscape gardens and pebble mosaic

COLFS, ALAIN AND KATE
Queensland, Australia
Web: www.wildash.com.au
email: wildash@halenet.com.au
Community projects and commissions
in pebble and glass

CURRIE, MARK
Lancashire, U.K.
email: markcurrie@btinternet.com
Pebble mosaics and ready-mades

EVELEIGH, DAVID
Herefordshire, U.K.
Web: www.goffee.co.uk
email: david@goffee.co.uk
Commissions for land art and mazes

HOWARTH, MAGGY
Cobblestone Designs
Lancaster, U.K.
Web: www.maggyhowarth.co.uk
email: maggy@maggyhowarth.co.uk
Pebble mosaics, workshops and
tutorial DVD

IRELAND, JANETTE
Lancashire, U.K.
Web: www.mosaicart.uk.com
email: janetteireland@aol.com
Pebble mosaics

IŞIKI, MEHMET
Meandr Handcraft
Antalya, Turkey
Web: www.meandrcraft.com
email: info@meandrcraft.com

KRETZMEIER, MARK
Oregon, U.S.
Web: www.metamosaics.com
email: info@metamosaics.com
Commissions for pebble mosaics

LOUKIANOS, YIANNIS
Athens, Greece
Web: www.pebblemosaics.gr
email: info@pebblemosaics.gr
Traditional Greek pebble mosaics,
restoration and lectures

MONRO, CHARLIE
Edinburgh, U.K.
email: charlie_monro@yahoo.com
Pebble mosaics and garden design

NERY, EDUARDO
Lisbon, Portugal
Web: www.eduardonery@clix.pt
email: eduardonery@clix.pt
Specialist in Portuguese cut-stone
mosaic

REW, SUE
Warwickshire, U.K.
email: sue.rew@btinternet.com
Pebble mosaics

SCHOLES, ANDREA
Midlothian, U.K.
Web: www.andreascholesdesigns.co.uk
email: andreascholes@hotmail.com
Pre-cast pebble mosaic and garden
design

SENŞOY, SINAN
Matusan, Istanbul, Turkey
Web: www.matusan.com
email: info@matusan.com
Pebble mosaics and pebble tiles;
vertical and flat

SHANGHAI LANDSCAPE ARCHITECTURE
DESIGN INSTITUTE
Web: www.shlandscape.com
email: ylsjy@shlandscape.com

SIEGERS, ULA
Neiderkrüchten, Germany
Web: www.kieselmosaik.de
email: ula@kieselmosaik.de
Miniature pebble mosaics and reliefs

STONE, LAURA
Minnesota, U.S.
Web: laurastonemosaics.com
email: kniferiver264@yahoo.com
Pebble mosaics

TESTER, ROB
London, U.K.
email: robtester@hotmail.com
Pebble mosaics

THOMPSON, KAREN
California, U.S.
Web: www.archetile.com
email: archetile@comcast.net
Mosaics in all media

ÜMMÜHAN, INCI
Istanbul, Turkey
email: ummuhaninci@gmail.com
Commissions for wall mosaics

VIELMETTER, JOHANNES
Bramsche, Germany
Web: www.vielmettermosaik.de
email: info@vielmettermosaik.de
Commissions for stone paintings

WACHSMUTH, ARIANE
Bilthoven, Netherlands
Web: www.kieselmozaiek.nl
email: ariane@wachsmuth.nl
Pebble mosaics

GENERAL INDEX

PHOTO CREDITS

The author would like to thank all those who supplied photographs.

ALDO, DEB 187; ANDERSEN, GLEN pages 154; ARCHAEOLOGICAL RECEIPTS FUND, ATHENS pages 91, 92, 216; BAKER, JOEL pages 158, 159, 139; BALE, JEFFREY back cover (top), pages 146, 147, 148, 149; BOTICA, JOHN pages 172, 173, 174, 175; CLARKE, WENDY 171; CLEVELAND ARTS page 212 (bottom right); COLFS, ALAIN 168, 169, 170; CORBETT, VAL front cover, half title page, pages 8, 20 (bottom), 41, 45, 50, 57 (top left), 161 (bottom), 167 (top right), 190–191, 202–203, 224, 228, 229, 237; DARRAH, GEZA cover (spine), 150, 151; DESMOND, CHRISTINE pages 87 (top right), 144–145, 217; DEWEY, WILLIAM B. page 113; EVELEIGH, DAVID pages 160, 188 (left); FORD, REBECCA 187 (top right); FREW, ROD 155, 254; HILL, JONATHAN page 164; HILL, JOSEPH, for Dumbarton Oaks Research Library & Collection page 112; HOW, TREVOR page 74 (bottom); IRELAND, JANETTE 185 (bottom), 162, 163; ISIKLI, MEHMET 83, 132, 133; JORDAN, LORNA 142; KRETZMEIER, MARK 153 (bottom left and right); LOUKIANOUS, YIANNIS pages 182, 183, 253; LANGRIDGE, JAQUI page 52; MCDONALD, DAVID pages 86–87, 143; MORRIS, ANDREW pages 78–79, 215 (left), 237 (top); NÉRY, ÉDUARDO page 97; REW, SUE 188 (bottom right); SCHOLES, ANDREA back cover (bottom right), 189 (bottom); SELF, BOB pages backcover (top), 152, 153 (top); SENSOY, SINAN pages 80, 81, 82, 124, 131; SHORT, EVERETT pages 98–99; SIEGERS, ULA 176, 177; STONE, LAURA 188 (top right); STORCK, DIETER pages 148 (bottom), 149, 182; THOMPSON, KAREN 187 (left); VIELMETTER, JOHANNES contents page (eagle), pages 178–181; WACHSMUTH, ARIANE 189 (top right); WATES, ROS page 161.

All other photos by BORIS & MAGGY HOWARTH.

◀ *An amazing mosaic by Mark Davidson in Western Park, Auckland, New Zealand, see also details on page 253 (bottom) and 254 (top). It's Mark's final work; a tour de force in his characteristic Polynesian-influenced style: a bold, flowing design of rolling waves, tree-fern leaves and sun motif. The size is extraordinary — this must be the largest pre-cast pebble mosaic yet.*